Becoming God's Friend

Becoming God's Friend

Understanding Your Growth from Servant to Friend

Jonathan Jenkins

Digital Bible Study Books
Houston | Atlanta

DEDICATION

To Mom and Dad,

This book is about the work of our heavenly Father. Nothing has prepared me more for writing it than having seen God's touch in the home you provided for our family. Without you, what follows could not have been written.

To Julie,

This book is about learning to trust in the power of another's love. Your ability to love me in spite of all my weaknesses and limitations is nothing short of Divine. Without you, what follows could not have been written.

To Eric,

This book is about the power of friendship to inspire us to believe that greatness is within our reach. Your example has shown me a glimpse of the infinite power of friendship with God. Without you, this book could not have been written.

The bird a nest

the spider a web

the human friendship

William Blake

TABLE OF CONTENTS

PREFACE

I had to talk to my father. I knew his advice would be the best. The counsel he gave me on that humid South Florida evening in June of 1992 changed my life forever. My heart was leading me to preach. There was no one who would know better than he did how to make that happen. I remember the discussion of that night well. I had seen the practiced and measured expressions on his face in the past. He was careful not to overstep and seem to be pushing too hard in the talk.

By that time he had already been a gospel preacher for nearly 40 years. We are a preaching family. His brother, two nephews, one cousin, his father and grandfather and easily a dozen other men in our family over the last few generations spent at least a portion of their lives preaching.

My father has three sons. I am the youngest. I am sure he had thought of the possibility of one of his sons following in his footsteps. No matter their profession, most fathers have the thought of their children emulating them. He never openly voiced that desire. I do not remember one time that he expressed an expectation that any of us would be preachers. There were daily expressions of the expectation that we would be faithful Christians. Preaching and preachers were held up as examples and role-models in our home. However, we were never pushed to preach just because he had.

His only daughter married a missionary and spent twenty years ministering in Kenya. His other two sons have served as elders and deacons in churches for years. I knew that he was (and is) proud of each one of us regardless of whether or not any of us ever followed in his steps and preached.

Yet his face struggled to hide the happiness in his heart that night. My dad has helped countless young men become preachers. Growing up, there was a steady stream of men leaving churches where he preached to go receive formal training in ministry. I know that his example and influence was largely responsible for that. He had engaged in the conversation we were having that night many times before. This time the circumstance was different. I was his son. There is something special about a father being able to share himself with his son. After a lifetime of service, he had a wealth of knowledge about preaching. Now he would be able to give that to his son.

That process of sharing changes things. All of his children have close and open relationships with him, but he and I have something they will never experience with him. There is a part of our lives that we share in a way that they cannot know. I can pick up the phone and express in just a few words a sentiment about the work of an evangelist that they could never fully understand no matter how long the conversation. He and I have a shared experience. We stand where the other stands. Our sharing has changed the relationship.

He is still my father. I am still his son. No issue of life will ever change that, but the bond of sharing we have in preaching has made him uniquely my friend. My wife will always be my closest friend, but when it comes to the joys and hardships of preaching, I call him first. When I seek advice on a biblical matter or on how to handle an issue in the church where I preach, his is often the only counsel I seek. I do not do it as a son. My call to him is not with a sense of duty or obligation. I cannot remember the last time I feared my father's anger. I know that if he ever said, "Son, do _____, now," that whatever went in that blank, I would do whatever I could to obey him. He is my father. "Children obey your parents in the Lord" has no expiration date on it. I know who he is; I know who I am; and I know the submissive interaction of those two facts. Yet that reality has no real motivational power in our relationship. Our bond is one of communion. My training at his hand has made our hearts to beat in harmony. From disuse, the specter of discipline has faded into the nothingness of memory.

I covet his counsel because I know he can be trusted. I seek it because I know he will always seek what is best for me. He knows what is right and almost always knows what is best and will share that wisdom with me freely. I reach out to him because I know his joy or sadness will be just as real and just as powerful as mine. I need him because he is my friend.

Jonathan

ACKNOWLEDGMENTS

The prospect of writing this section of *Becoming God's Friend* has been a source of hope throughout this endeavor. Writing these words means the work of creation is done. If it is possible to feel love and hate at the same time, I have held on to both in creating this study. The study and contemplation of God and His great man of faith in Abraham, I have loved in every moment. The hope that maybe someone struggling in his faith would be encouraged not only to hold on but also to grow closer to God after reading this book has lifted my spirit at all times. Finding subject and verb disagreements, worrying about whether to use a comma or colon, and a thousand other issues of grammar and formatting is not an endeavor for which I have any affection. I can honestly say that I have hated each of those moments. All of that means that there is a long list people that need to be thanked. Without their help, this book would have never be finished.

First, I need to thank the members of the Avondale church of Christ and the Katy church of Christ. Each in their own turn participated in the classes and sermons where this material was first presented. Your input, criticisms, and encouragement helped make this work into what it is.

Second, I need to express my gratitude for those people who helped in proofing and editing the material. Mickie Warriner and Jim Taylor read through the earliest editions of the manuscript that were too jumbled to hand over to the final editor. Their contributions were invaluable to me. The hard task of final edits was accomplished by Laura Winckler. She corrected my wayward grammar and syntax with a soft touch even as her ink spread freely over my manuscript.

Thank you to each one of you. May God be praised by our efforts.

INTRODUCTION

"What is a friend? A single soul dwelling in two bodies."
Aristotle

Following my father's counsel, in August of 1992 I arrived at the school I had chosen to attend to help prepare me to preach the gospel. I enrolled in a small school for preachers in Memphis aptly named The Memphis School of Preaching. The class with which I started only had about 20 men in it. In that group, there were a good number of men with whom I appeared to have much in common. There was another son of a preacher in the class. Coming from a preaching home is a strong point of connection. We both had a good understanding of what the life we were undertaking meant. He seemed like someone I would get to know well. Early on, I met another student who shared much of my background in other areas. We had both grown up in the South. We shared a passion for baseball and so had suffered through the horrible 1980's of the Atlanta Braves. Together in my home, we watched Sid Bream slide across home in the ninth inning to win game seven of the 1993 National League Championship Series. He too seemed like someone who would be a life-long friend. In even such a small class, there were several men with whom I seemed to have a common footing.

Then there was Eric. On the surface, we shared very little. I had grown up in the South. His home was Rockford, Illinois. I come from that long line of preachers. He was the first in his family. In 1992, he was just back from Kuwait and his service as a Marine in Desert Storm. My family has little background in military service. He played college basketball and was on the All-Marine basketball team. I was more at home in a computer lab. He is an African-American. I am as white as we come. Two peas in a pod we were not.

None of us in the class knew each other, so the class' dynamics took a few weeks to become apparent. I spent some time with the fellow preacher's son and with my baseball friend. While I still consider them friends today and we stay in contact with each other, the common points we share failed to create a truly deep friendship.

I do not remember my first conversation with Eric. Our bond grew quickly because it was soon apparent that we shared something much deeper than our surface differences. We were both serious about the work we were doing at the school, and we were both intensely competitive.

Every chance we found we were pushing each other. If we walked up the stairs together, it was a race (He won most of them.). There was no need to announce it – we both knew. We kept a running tally of victories on the ping-pong table in the school's break room (He won there, too.). We wasted hours of time we should have been studying trying to defeat each other on a computer golf game we had (He won more than he lost.). If we were in an activity together, it was a contest. Our competition extended to our schoolwork. We pushed each other every step of the way. The grading scale and the other students did not matter. We had our own mission. We pushed each other to finish first and second in our class (Let's just say, he didn't finish first.). Our attachment made us better and brought us closer.

Competition sometimes breeds enemies. We were not competitors. We were friends. Instead of trying to beat the other person down, we fed off each other's energy and commitment. To this day, we rejoice at each other's successes and are built up and inspired by the other's example. We found something unexpected in each other. Our backgrounds and appearances did not hint at it. Even our personalities are far different from each other. Yet, our friendship's power has changed my life and his.

Friendship is powerful. The strength of its bond has the ability to get past everything that seems to be important and find the things that are truly important. Those things are never external. They always deal with the spirit. They are shared values and goals. Friendship is about who you truly are, not who you appear to be.

The bond of friendship is among the greatest blessings God has given to man. In this world, friends are the bedrock to our sense of identity and belonging. The security and tenderness of the shared connection with a dear friend gives limitless strength and peace. In the intimacy of those special relationships there is no fear of failure or rejection or scorn. Our dreams are free to grow bigger and they seem nearer our grasp when they are nurtured in the warmth of friendship. The best friends that I have in my life enrich and encourage me. I can do more and be more because of them. They guide and inspire me. My friends trust me. They allow me to fail and lift me up when I do. I need and love them in the best and worst of times. I am better because of the bond I share with them than I could ever be on my own.

People simply need friends.

Friendship is Dangerous

You likely have people in your life like Eric is in my life – but I doubt you have many of them. True friendship is an elusive ideal. Finding someone that can be fully brought into such an intimate and trusted relationship is almost impossibly hard.

Think about how many people have passed through your life that at the time seemed essential to it. Growing up, we have many "best friends." As we age, they fall away one by one only to be replaced by others. Andy, Leslie, Scott, Ryan, Jason, Chris, and Daryl are all names of people that were special to me at one time. During the last twenty years, I have only spoken to one of them. Life moved on and friendships were lost.

However, staying in contact with a loved one does not guarantee friendship. Sometimes even after reaching that loved one, he still does not connect with us emotionally. Our hearts are hurting or bursting with joy. We are reaching out with a rush of emotion to a dear companion and in response there is apathy or scorn. Maybe the relationship was not as strong as we thought. The loved one may be so overwhelmed in his own emotions that he missed the passion of ours. He may have just misunderstood or misinterpreted the intensity of our feelings. The causes are almost limitless, but little hurts more than missing a needed connection with a loved one.

Then there is the permanent disruption of our connections that our mortality places upon us. Even the closest friends, companions and spouses will say goodbye to each other at some point. We spend a lifetime building those intimate bonds and just as they are at their strongest and we have grown the most dependent upon them, death comes and takes them away from us forever.

Solomon expressed this vulnerability inherent in friendship. He wrote, "A man of many companions may come to ruin, but there is a friend who sticks closer than a brother" (Proverbs 18:24). Entrusting too many people with the privilege of friendship leads to pain and often betrayal. Solomon said even more in that verse. His affirmation is that there is "a friend" that sticks closer than a brother. This bond is personal and intimate. By its very nature, if it is shared too broadly it is lost. Friendship must be exclusive for it to be powerful and secure.

Fulfilling our need for a true friend is among the most dangerous choices we will ever make. Fear of being betrayed or abandoned keeps many of us from fully taking the risk of becoming true friends with another. So we quietly suffer through this emotional isolation with only the meager solace of passing acquaintances whom we call friends to aide us.

If only there were a friend who was always worthy of the trust needed in friendship.

God – The Friend Closer Than a Brother

There is one place where all the joys of being and having a true friend can be explored without all the dangers that threaten friendship. Yet, it is the one place that so many of us seem reluctant to consider. We even go so far as to doubt whether or not we are allowed to dream that we belong there. That place is in relationship of friendship with God.

The reasons we hesitate to think of being God's friend are numerous and understandable. God is holy and infinite. We are not and never will be. We always come short of His glorious call on our lives (Romans 3:23). In a comparison with God, feeling anything other than inadequacy is impossible. When life is indecipherable and sin is overwhelming, we are driven to think that our best leaves God wanting more from us. We hear the great promises of abundant life and the abiding presence of our shepherding Lord; however, we struggle to experience the realization of that power. We are pressed to interpret that sense of emptiness as our inability to live up to God's will for our lives.

We can scarcely imagine having God as close and as common as a friend. Servants are submissive to masters. Sons are submissive to fathers. We are submissive to God. Friendship is maintained between peers and we are not His equals. There must always remain a distance between us. In that gap created by His perfection and our limitations, there is room for all of the angst and fear that shadows His face from us. That dynamic would seem to eliminate from discussion the idea that we can be God's friends.

Aristotle defined friendship by saying, "What is a friend? A single soul dwelling in two bodies." How could we ever believe that we are that "single soul" with God when His thoughts are not our thoughts and His ways are not our ways (Isaiah 55:8-9)?

That inhibition has a tragic effect on our lives. Our experience with the vagaries of human frailty conditions us to protect our hearts from too much intimacy with others. Our self-image as unworthy and lacking before God keeps us from fulfilling our need for connection in the only Being that can be trusted without restraint. It is no wonder so many people wander through life shrouded in the mist of their hearts' loneliness.

Yet, the promise of such an empowering connection with God is revealed in the pages of His word. His presence should encourage you to explore all the potential that He has placed within you, not paralyze your heart out of the fear of taking a wrong step. The thought of God's watching over you should sharpen your focus on the limitless good that can be done with your life, not encumber your hopes of what could be. The bond you have with God is intended to lift you and make you more than you could be without it. If understanding God's presence in your life fills you with guilt and shame and doubt, there is more that you need to know about God.

True friendship should be seen nowhere more clearly than with God. He is "the" Friend that will stick closer than a brother. His faithfulness will never disappoint, never fail, never betray, and never violate the trust He is given. God's love is pure and is never selfish or manipulative. He is never petty or vain. His offer of friendship is the offer of a relationship that will change your life forever.

Through His promises in Christ, we have been brought into the deepest affections of the heart of God. We have been elevated far above mere servants destined to a life of mindless routine. Our spirits are protected in His care and have been entrusted to dream of spiritual victories. We have been given the liberty to fail without being cast off. Ours is to be a life lived without fear. He has invited us into a relationship of complete openness. God is asking us to become that 'single soul dwelling in two bodies' with Him. More than that, I believe He has already laid out the path by which we can reach such an amazing pinnacle of faith. Someone has gone before us.

In the Bible, friendship with God is most clearly explained in the life of one man. Three times Abraham is called the "friend of God" (1 Chronicles 20:7; Isaiah 41:8; James 2:23). He is the only individual that is ever directly assigned that description. Abraham's life of faith with God moved him into a treasured place of intimacy with his Lord. He had been taken into the inner most regions of God's heart and walked so closely to his Lord that God freely took him into His council, "Shall I hide from Abraham what I am about to do?" (Genesis 18:17). His friendship with God was more than just a master and servant. God was Abraham's companion, and he was God's.

While Abraham is alone in having that title of "the friend of God," he does receive it. His friendship with God and his success in that relationship means it is possible. I know friendship with God is within my reach and yours. Abraham's success shows us that it is possible.

Faith Fulfilled Ends In Friendship

When we consider Abraham's life, the defining quality that comes to our minds is faith. Abraham is the "father of the faithful" and the "father of all who believe." He is, at the same time, the example of how a man is saved by faith "apart from his works" (Romans 4:6) and the example of how "faith is completed by works" (James 2:21-22). Abraham serves as the archetype of faith that God wants us to see.

Yet, as we just noted, he is also uniquely described as God's friend. We should not be surprised then, that the concepts of faith and friendship are joined together in Abraham. The man who is the pattern of our faith is also the pattern of our friendship with God.

The connection between friendship and faith is natural and intuitive. At its most basic level, friendship is simple trust. The more I trust another's heart and intentions toward me, the more I am willing to give of myself to Him. He, in turn, learns to trust my heart and intentions toward him. This cycle of deepening faith will continue to draw our hearts closer together and more secure in our connection until our investment of faith is betrayed or neglected. Faith deposited into a worthy companion has within it the greatest of promises. When that faith is grown to its fulfillment, you will find a true friend.

This powerful dynamic of faith in a growing friendship is exactly what the Bible reveals happened between Abraham and God. The journey of Abraham's life is the perfect highlight that we need to discover how placing our trust in God's companionship introduces us to the greatest friendship we will ever know.

God's lingering work with Abraham succeeded in fulfilling his faith when he so freely trusted his relationship with God that his heart was free to open itself so that nothing within it was hidden from God. Not even his only son, for whom he had waited for over 20 years, stood between God and Abraham. God's praise of His friend at that offering shows how special He knew Abraham's gift of Isaac was:

> By myself I have sworn, declares the LORD, because you have done this and have *not withheld your son, your only son*, I will surely bless you, and I will surely multiply your offspring as the stars of Heaven and as the sand that is on the seashore. And your offspring shall possess the gate of his enemies. (Genesis 22:16-17)

Abraham's whole life was opened for his Friend. There was no distance between them. Abraham had overcome the gap of intimacy that we so often feel between us and our God. Abraham became the friend of God when faith removed from his heart all of the obstacles between them. At Isaac's altar, Abraham knew that God would provide a lamb for the offering because he knew that his Friend would never betray him. With the barriers in Abraham's heart broken down, no obstacle held them apart. God had brought His man of faith to a point of intimacy that could only be called . . . friendship:

Was not Abraham our father justified by works when he offered up his son Isaac on the altar . . . and the Scripture was fulfilled that says, "Abraham believed God, and it was counted to him as righteousness" – and he was called a friend of God. (James 2:21-23)

I hope to convince you in the pages of this book that God wants to secure your heart in the bond of that same friendship. If you cannot see yourself in that light now, please do not worry. Fulfilling the promise residing in your faith takes time. It did for Abraham. His journey was hard and yours will be also.

Friendship is never easy. While the choices of Abraham's faith will seem unattainable at some points, remember, they were made during three decades of his walking with God. He is an old man, marked by all the scars of life, by the time he lifts his hand up to offer Isaac. His life has been full of all of the ups and downs one would expect. His faith has been challenged from the first step out of Ur to the last step to Isaac's body, prone on the altar. Let us not make light of this. Following Abraham in his journey to God is no small task. This kind of friendship is not made as easily as picking up a book, reading it and having your life changed.

The need for growth in Abraham's faith teaches that no man starts his walk with God as God's friend. Faith must be grown. Like friendship, faith develops in stages and deepens the longer it exists. But the growth potential inherent in faith means that every man can become a dear friend of God just like Abraham. God is not looking for some ability that only exists in a select few or in the spiritual giants of the world. Faith produces friendship and faith is within the reach of each person. From the moment a man's heart recognizes his need for God, that seed of faith has within it the potential to walk in the steps of trust that Abraham's life places in front of us. That seed of faith is bearing fruit in your heart right now. Your faith, just like Abraham's, can be fulfilled in friendship with God.

A Starting Question

Have you ever asked yourself: "What is God's plan for me?"

Most Christians have, in one form or another. If you have, then your beginning point in this study can be highlighted in understanding why you asked this question.

To ask that question, you must have been faced with a choice, or perhaps a crisis of faith. In that moment the impulse of your heart was to consider what God would want from you. Seeking God's guidance in trial is wonderful. However, I am convinced, that question is asked out of two antithetical motivations. One is out of fear. The other is out of hope. One Christian asks it because he is worried that by making the "wrong choice," God will be displeased with him and his salvation will be threatened. The other Christian asks it because he is convinced in finding the "right choice," God will lead him to greater spiritual victories. One saint sees in God the potential to fail. The other sees in God the promise of triumph. One is God's servant. The other is becoming God's friend. Which one are you?

Earlier, we made some statements about the impact of friends on our lives. Friends encourage and inspire and challenge us to be more. They believe in us even when we fail. We take refuge in the strength their unwavering commitment to us provides. Can you honestly say that about your relationship with God? Is His call on your life an opportunity to explore and experience the best your life and faith can offer or is His call for you a task that must be completed? Perhaps, the truth of your existence is somewhere in between.

This study is not about God. He is infinite and perfect. We will not be studying the power of the blood of Christ. Its power is intrinsic and enduring. This study is about you and what you believe that you can be with God. I want you to examine your view of the expansiveness and terms of God's blessings. In short, our study is not focused on reality; rather, our concern is over our perception of that reality. The reality is that God has saved you; God loves you; and God will provide you all the opportunity you can receive in this life. Whether we believe it or not, the path into the depths of His heart has been cleared of every obstacle. What determines how far you walk into those depths is your perception of what God has made available to you. You will only travel as far as you believe that God has deemed you worthy to go.

The growth to which you are being called in this study is the walk of your lifetime. This journey has only one end. The last step on the path takes you into eternity to be with your Friend. Be patient with yourself as you walk – God is. Be patient. Growing closer to God than you have ever been is a difficult journey.

God is calling you out of Ur into a land of promise and hope; a land of communion between dear friends. Join me, as we embark upon this journey together. You can become a friend of God!

PART 1 - FROM SERVANT TO FRIEND

What does it mean to "be God's friend?"

To answer that, we should first consider a few things it does not mean:

- Someone is not saved until they are God's friend.
- Someone's salvation is in doubt until they are God's friend.
- Someone's commitment or faithfulness should be doubted until they are God's friend.

We are studying our view of our relationship to God, not the strength of God's promises regarding us. Every blessing of intimacy that God has to offer to the saved is yours to enjoy from the moment the blood of Jesus washes you free from sin. That is the reality. Unfortunately, your perception of God and your place before Him can hinder your ability to live in the closeness He is offering you.

Part 1 of this book discusses four different images used in scripture to describe our relationship to God. The reality is that we are all of the things that follow – servant, steward, son, and friend – from the moment we are saved. How we choose to view ourselves will determine how we experience our faith.

Which of those terms best describes your walk with God? Let's find out together.

1

FROM SERVANT TO SON

The slave does not remain in the house forever; the son remains forever.
(John 8:35)

"I am God's _____."

Finish that sentence before reading any farther. What you place in that blank says a great deal about how you perceive your relationship to God. I would encourage you to limit your response to images that can be found in the Bible. Using Scripture's own language to express your faith whenever you can is always a good idea. It is the surest way to ensure that the idea you are conveying comes first from the mind of God.

Within the language of the Bible, you have a good number of words from which to select to complete that thought. Three come to mind immediately. They are good Bible words. Each one aptly describes an important concept about the kind of relationship we should have with Him. Those words are: servant, steward, and son.

I would not be surprised if any or all of those terms came to your mind as you read that sentence. They are found all over the Bible. I believe these terms can be rightly applied to any person who has a relationship with Him. In fact, all three of these ideas are true of us at all times. From the moment we become Christians, we become and never cease to be His servants, His stewards, and His sons. We are always all of these people in God's eyes.

We need to see all three of these facets of our relationship with Him. Each is purposefully used by God to help mold us into the kind of beings He wants us to be. There are times when the obligation of slavery strengthens us against rebellion. At other moments in life, the promise of stewardship encourages us to keep our eyes focused on the reward of Heaven. When life is difficult, only the intimate comfort of sonship can quiet our troubled hearts.

The challenge of harmonizing the varied facets of our relationship with God is within us. Some of us never grow in all of these areas. Some never learn the lessons of a servant and so will not submit to His authority. Others never embrace the opportunity of stewardship and their growth is stunted. More never believe that they are truly dear children of God and in so doing learn to trust that God is with them. The best-developed Christians never lose sight of any of these relationships.

We need to embrace the lessons each these of images adds to our faith.

I am God's Servant

The Bible's view of man is that of a servant. Every man has a master. God has given us the choice over who that master is, but we will have one. Our options are limited to two. We can give ourselves to be servants of sin or of obedience:

> Do you not know that if you present yourselves to anyone as obedient slaves, you are slaves of the one whom you obey, either of sin, which leads to death, or of obedience, which leads to righteousness? (Romans 6:16)

There is our choice: To whom will we give ourselves?

We who are Christians have chosen the harder path. Being a servant of sin is an easy choice to make as it requires no courage. Simple acquiescence to the world will lead one into the service of sin.

There are unwelcome consequences along the way and its destiny is hard, but the path is easy. Being a servant of obedience to God is much more difficult. An active movement of the will and a lifetime of commitment are required. Notice the distinction Jesus made about the narrow gate of service in God's kingdom and the wide gate of service to sin:

> Enter by the narrow gate. For the gate is wide and the way is easy that leads to destruction, and those who enter by it are many. For the gate is narrow and the way is hard that leads to life, and those who find it are few. (Matthew 7:13-14)

One gate is narrow and must be found. Effort is needed to enter there. The other gate is wide and the path down the road through it is easy in appearance. Being a servant of sin takes no courage, while being a servant of obedience to God is hard.

Why make the choice to serve God then? If the way is hard, why not choose the easier path? The answer for a servant is easy. At the end of the path of the narrow gate is life while at the end of the wide gate is death. Simple self-preservation motivates a servant to choose to please his master.

Servants serve their masters out of obligation. Their service is forced from the control of fear. The imagery of a servant of God is really no different. The most common Greek word translated "servant" in our English Bibles is the word "doulos." "Doulos" describes a slave – a bondman – one who is in a permanent relation of servitude to another (Trench 46). Paul emphasizes the nature of this relationship in 1 Corinthians 7:23, "You were bought with a price; do not become slaves of men." All servants of God have been purchased into His service with a price higher than any man-made slave in history: Jesus.

Underlying the service of every slave is the fear of punishment. When slaves disobey the master, they are punished as slaves. The servant in the "Parable of the Unjust Servant" (Matthew 18) was delivered to the jailors without compassion. The wicked servants of Matthew 24 who think the master is not coming back are cut into pieces at the master's unexpected return (v. 51). A slave has no rights in the master's house. Every day of his life is a day of service to please the master. If he fails, punishment is his fate.

We can never lose sight of that aspect of our relationship to God. We have been bought with a price and are owned by our Lord. The highest work that we can have is to so labor in His service that our work is done just as He envisioned it: "It is enough for the disciple to be like his teacher, and the servant like his master" (Matthew 10:25). No matter how much we grow or how long we live in God's service, we never cease to be under an obligation to serve as His slaves.

We must never forget that duty. But please, do not let your heart stop at slavery. We are far more than slaves. There are more images left as we think about our relationship to God. Christians who never move past the concept of themselves as the slaves of God are tragic figures. However, far too many remain there. They never get beyond measuring themselves by the amount of work that they have done. They hear the words of Jesus as He says, "So you also, when you have done all that you were commanded, say, 'We are unworthy servants; we have only done what was our duty'" (Luke 17:10). Out of the intricate tapestry woven in the Bible's words about our standing with God, they find that one thread and hear only that they are nothing more than unworthy servants.

These Christians are easy to spot. Their spiritual life resembles a hamster running on the wheel in its cage. There is motion. The activity is furious. But the wheel knows no end. They can never take a break. No time can be spared. There is no passion behind the activity. The fear of failure fuels their engine. Ask a Christian like this if he is saved or if he is going to Heaven, and you will not hear a resounding "yes" in praise of God. What you will hear is a response tempered by his uncertainty as he says, "If I remain faithful," or "I'm working on it." For the servant, his hope for Heaven is tied directly to his faith in himself. His hope can only be as strong as his faith in his own abilities to keep his master's commands. His relationship with God provides hope in that he can see Heaven, but it provides greater doubt because hell is forever closing in on him.

Thankfully, God has called us to more than slavery.

I am a God's Steward

From history, we know the concept of slavery well. Perhaps the meaning of stewardship is not as well known to us, nevertheless, the practice of hiring a steward was widespread in the ancient world. Ralph

Earle describes stewardship in these words: "The word comes from oikos, 'house,' and nemo, 'manage.' So it literally means 'a house manager. "Wealthy men employed slaves or freedmen to manage their households for them" (221).

While in Potiphar's house, Joseph serves as a good example of a house manager. Joseph is said to have been put over all that Potiphar had. He was trusted with all of Potiphar's goods to the degree that the Egyptian had no concern for the things of his house except for the food that he ate (Genesis 39:6). Joseph was his slave but was trusted in his service as a steward.

In the New Testament, at least two parables touch on the idea of stewardship. The "Parable of the Talents" (Matthew 25:14-30) describes three servants who are made stewards. In fact, these men are called "slaves" ("doulos") in the parable. When the master departs he gives his treasure ("talents") into the charge of his servants. Once charged with the oversight of a portion of their master's goods, they become stewards. They are given responsibility and the freedom to manage those goods. Two succeed and one fails. Two are rewarded and their roles expanded. One fails and is punished for his unfaithful service.

The second parable is the "Parable of the Unjust Steward" (Luke 16:1-13). There, a steward over a rich man's possessions had been wasting the treasures under his charge. When the report comes back to the master, he calls his steward in to give an account of his actions. The steward knows he is in trouble and is soon to be expelled from his role. In an act of self-preservation, he calls the master's debtors and massages the books in their favor in hopes that when he is expelled, the debtors will look favorably upon him. In his own words he said, "What shall I do, since my master is taking the management away from me? I am not strong enough to dig, and I am ashamed to beg" (16:3). What we learn about stewardship in this parable is the responsibility given to a steward. In this instance, the man was not worthy of the job, but that he could so freely misuse the master's possessions shows the freedom he had been given.

Stewards are trusted servants. They are servants with an opportunity to advance and grow. The successful stewards in the "Parable of the Talents" are told, "You have been faithful over little; I will set you over much" (Matthew 25:21, 23). Their faithful service granted to them more responsibility and more reward. In that sense, stewards serve not out of a fear of punishment but in the hope of reward.

The promise of remuneration separates them from being just slaves. Both servant and steward are slaves. Their positions are both subject to the judgment of the master. The fearful, one-talent steward who did not increase his master's goods was punished as harshly as any other evil servant. Before that, he was given a chance to grow as his own abilities would allow. There is no expectation and little opportunity for a slave to do the same.

Stewards then are invested in this process of growth. The master wants more from them than blind service. He wants their creativity. The master placed his talents in the hand of his servants in expectation that they would increase his wealth. He wanted more from them than just the interest his monies could have gotten in the "bank." His monies working together with their energies was the path to the stewards' reward.

In the same manner, Paul understood the work of an apostle of Christ was the work of stewardship, "This is how one should regard us, as servants of Christ and stewards of the mysteries of God" (1 Corinthians 4:1). He knew that God had specially entrusted the apostles and prophets of the early church with the greatest of God's treasures. They had been given the gospel of Jesus Christ and charged with the mission of spreading it to the world. Those chosen men were slaves in His service. More than slaves, they were provided an opportunity to grow the master's wealth by the preaching of His precious treasure.

Paul's application of the imagery of stewardship shaped his work as an apostle. He knew his role was to please the judgment of the master because he understood what was required of a steward (4:2). What another besides his Master thought of his work was irrelevant. Even Paul's own evaluation of his life was of little consequence to this steward. All that matters to a steward is whether or not the master is pleased (4:3-4). As a steward, Paul was working and waiting for one thing – the pronouncement of God's approval of his service:

Therefore do not pronounce judgment before the time, before the Lord come, who will bring to light the things now hidden in darkness and will disclose the purposes of the heart. Then each one will receive his commendation from God. (4:5)

We, too, are stewards of God. The growth of His glory in this world is placed in our hands. Each of us has his own work. We have our own place of service. While those roles differ, God expects the same of each of us. He expects that we will use our own abilities, creativity, and energy to make more of the opportunities He gives us.

Stewardship is a higher calling than just slavery. Stewardship's calling means that God trusts us to do His will. He has always trusted man. The angels of Heaven marveled that God had placed man over the works of His hands:

> What is man that you are mindful of him, and the son of man that you care for him? Yet you have made him a little lower than the heavenly beings and crowned him with glory and honor. You have given him dominion over the works of your hands; you have put all things under his feet. (Psalm 8:4-6)

Despite their confusion, God did trust those He made in His image. He gave man the garden and said, "Keep it." He sent man into a world ravaged by the flood and said, "Refill it." He gave man the gospel of salvation and said, "Preach it." He gave you your life and said, "Live it." You have a high place in God's will.

Yet, we are called to a higher standing with God. Stewards are still just servants. Joseph was sent to prison. The Unjust Steward was removed and punished. The One-Talent Steward was cast into outer darkness. As high as stewardship is, if the steward fails the master, he will be replaced. We are His stewards and will always be called to trusted service. Still, there is more to come. We are more than house managers.

This place of management is a resting place and even end point for the faith of many Christians They rest in stewardship because they see little more than reward and punishment. A steward has a hope of reward, but that is the highest motivation of his calling. If faithful in service, his role can be increased, but he will still be a servant. A Christian focused on the potential of his failure – and so on Hell – will never be more than a slave for God. A Christian focused only on his reward – and so on Heaven – will never be more than a steward.

These Christians are easy to spot. They may trust that Heaven is their reward, but their eyes can see only what Heaven will provide for them. Ask them why they are serving God and the answer likely has to do with their own needs and how Heaven will meet them. They will speak of the removal of death, sorrow, and pain that Heaven will provide. The longing in their hearts to be reunited with loved ones in eternity is powerful.

There is nothing at all wrong with those desires for Heaven and reunion. They are the reward of faithful stewardship. However, service done for those blessings is still service done based on accounting principles. "I serve God so that I will receive" is the metric of a steward. The Unjust Steward served his master because he was too weak to dig and too proud to beg. What the master provided was better than life without his provisions. So, the Unjust Steward served. Many Christians serve at this same level. They serve in view of the reward. They serve because the alternative is unthinkable.

Stewardship is powerful and important in our lives. However understood properly, the simple management of stewardship is still too limited and limiting for what God has promised us. If there were not more, then we could hope for nothing more than glorified slavery in God's house. We could never rise above reward and punishment.

Thankfully, God has called us to more than stewardship.

I am God's Son

Beyond stewardship, sonship comes into view. The divide between the two separates service and love. Living between father and son there is love. This connection does not exist even with the best of stewards. Joseph was trusted and cherished by Potiphar only as long as Joseph increased Potiphar's wealth. Despite all of his faithful service, no love existed between Joseph and his master. There is no love needed between master and servant. In the souls of father and son, love makes all the difference. The father of the Prodigal Son longed and watched for the return of his son. Their separation and the offences wrought by the Prodigal would have brought judgment upon the most productive servant. Nevertheless, when the son returned, the father's love restored him. Sonship is the heat that melds obedience with fellowship.

All servants are focused on obedience. Their task is to do what the master has said. A son also obeys his father, but that obedience is just the beginning. His obedience is the commencement of his fellowship and communion with his father. A servant has to earn his standing every day. A son has a birthright. From the moment he enters the world, the father is obligated to care for him. Any man that ignores that fact, God views as more despised than an unbeliever (1 Timothy 5:8). The father has a duty to train, discipline, and love his son at all times. No offence can ever blur the line between slaves and sons.

We have been called into sonship. This intimate family relationship fills the pages of the New Testament. From the giving of the "Model Prayer" in the "Sermon on the Mount" when we are instructed to call God our "Father," to Paul's firm assertion to the Galatians that we "are the sons of God" (Galatians 4:6), to John's amazement that the great expression of love that God has given that "we should be called the children of God" (1 John 3:1), God wants us to know that we are His beloved children. By bringing us into that relationship with Him, He has promised us His care, His guidance, His discipline, and His love. We are His family.

How does that change us? Is not the job of a son, very much like the job of servant? In many ways it is. In fact, the growth and maturation of a son very much mimics the progression of the relationship that we have been discussing in this chapter. Consider Paul's statement about the relationship of sons and servants:

> I mean that the heir, as long as he is a child, is no different from a slave, though he is the owner of everything, but he is under guardians and managers until the date set by his father. (Galatians 4:1-2)

A son in his youth is no different than a servant. Why does that child serve or obey his father? His service is motivated very much like that of a "doulos" or a slave. A slave serves to keep the master's punishment from coming to him. The first impulse of a child's obedience to a parent differs little.

I remember that process of training with my children quite well. That the wheels in their minds were spinning in trying to determine whether or not to obey my command was written right on their faces. Whether or not they obeyed was not motivated out of some well-developed sense of love or respect. No, that young child obeys or disobeys based on the belief he has about the certainty of punishment. His service is little different from that of a slave.

21

As the son grows, the relationship changes. His capacity to love and honor begins to grow. However, in a young adolescent, love is still not the primary motivation of service. Parents begin to treat that growing son more like a steward. He is given chores around the house. He is given areas of responsibility to manage in the home. The child's task may be putting laundry away or cleaning his room or taking out the trash or a thousand other tasks. Two things happen as he does his chores. He grows in responsibility and is challenged with more opportunities to work. He is also rewarded. He is given an allowance or privileges in the home. Good parents begin to show the child the place of a good work ethic in his life. Once that child starts receiving an allowance, what is the common response? Like most of us when it comes to money, he wants more. He begins to serve for reward. Sure, other things are happening. Absolutely, he is learning lessons of respect and love toward his parents. Yet, those lessons are the desires of the parents, not the motivation of the child. He just wants his allowance. In his youth, there is little difference between a son and steward. Both of them serve to be rewarded.

Roll the clock forward a few years and see that son as a teenager or young adult. Yes, he still is bound to his father in service. If he is still in the home, he may be reaping reward for his work. Yet why is this young man serving his father? At some point, his service stops being focused inwardly. His service becomes one motivated by his concern for his father instead of himself. He seeks to show his love and respect. His service has changed.

The slave serves out of obligation. The steward serves for reward. The son serves to honor. He wants to honor his father and show his father his appreciation for all that has been done for him. Seeing his father grieved at his failure would be as great a punishment to the son as the father's wrath. Nearly every child has a moment like that. When, after having hurt a parent in making a wrong choice, he longs for punishment. Instead, the disappointed parent just sits in silence with his faced lined in the creases only a broken heart can leave. If you have ever experienced that pain, you know the difference between sonship and stewardship.

All through my teenage years, I can remember hearing my father say to me as I left the house, "Remember who you are." There was no long list of do's and do not's. I was supposed to know those already. His message was just a simple, but powerful reminder of the standards set for our family. He was calling on my developing sense of honor for the example he had set to guide me. His words were a call to honor.

A good son cannot imagine dishonoring his father. The greatest son of all knew this and lived by it. One of Jesus' earliest statements in the Bible stated this understanding plainly. "I must be in my Father's house" (Luke 2:49). "I must," He said. There was no other choice. That statement does not hint at the fear of a slave or the outcome-based service of a steward. Those words are uttered by one that knows who He is. Being God's son means that God must be honored in His life. As an adult, Jesus' sentiment was the same. He told His disciples, "My food is to do the will of him who sent me and to accomplish his work" (John 4:34). His life was focused on working in harmony with the desires of His Father. As He approached death, His focus was still on honoring His Father. He promised His disciples that He would respond to their requests because He wanted His Father to be glorified in His life, "Whatever you ask in my name, this I will do, that the Father may be glorified in the Son" (John 14:13). A dozen more examples from the Savior's life could be added. His was a service as a son that was wholly focused on the exaltation of His Father.

Sonship is indeed a high calling from God. The fellowship that sonship creates with our Creator elevates our lives and draws us close to Him. We are released from the burden of slavery and the uncertainty of stewardship. In God's house, we now live as family members. We are truly freed from this world and from sin. Our lives add a personal touch to the glory that is our new family name. Even with all of His majesty and with all of the ways He is showing His glory in this world, our sonship gives us the chance to partake in and increase His honor. Sonship is an amazing privilege.

There are many Christians who do live their lives as sons. Their lives and faith are transformed from slavery. A servant is always worried about the judgment of the master. A son with a good father is never worried that the judgment of his father will take away his sonship. Jesus made this promise to His disciples, "The slave does not remain in the house forever; the son remains forever. So if the Son sets you free, you will be free indeed" (John 8:35-36). A son knows that no matter how he fails or struggles; he is still a son. Even if he turns, denounces his father and walks away, like the Prodigal, he can come back. A good father always loves his son and God is *the* good Father.

Christians such as these are easy to spot. Ask them about their salvation and God will be praised. His name will be exalted. Ask them why they serve and they will express His love and His grandeur in their answer. Their service is freely given. The work they do is the true expression of a heart longing to lift up God. Reward and punishment are not in the picture – only God.

Servant, Steward or Son?

Remember from the introduction, we stated this is a study about perception and not reality. In finding yourself in the three biblical images we discussed in this chapter the issue is not whether or not you *are* a servant, steward or son. You are all of those before Him. The issue is which imagery dominates your daily life and is the motivation of your faith.

What is important is not that you never again see yourself as God's servant. For every person of faith, the black and white clarity of servanthood will always provide a bedrock layer of strength in your faithfulness to God. What is important is that you can occasionally scale the ladder to sonship. If you cannot understand your sonship with God or if you are permanently locked into the life of a lowly servant, your faith and ultimately your salvation could be in jeopardy. The servant will face crises of faith that he has no power to overcome without the blessings of sonship. Moving "down" this ladder is easy for the son. He knows how to live as a servant; he has lived that way before. However, moving "up" this ladder for the servant is impossible until his faith can see more.

The question to ask yourself then, is not "Am I a servant, steward, or son?" The question of significance is "Do I feel like a servant, steward or son?" When you approach God in prayer and in the daily walk of your faith, in which of these images is your faith most comfortably wrapped?

2

FROM SON TO FRIEND

"You're a man now, son."

Every son looks forward to the day that his father utters those words to him. Those words are a commission of approval. The father is proud of his son. The son is trusted. A new phase in the relationship of father and son has begun. The man who was once a teacher and disciplinarian is now a counselor and companion. While a son is growing up, his father cannot afford to offer his son friendship. The degree of intimacy that comes with friendship spoils a child and ruins his respect for his father. At some point, that period of training reaches its end. The boy becomes a man. The father becomes a friend.

I remember the first time that sentiment was expressed in a real way to me by my father. He had said it at all the appropriate times as I grew. However, I am not talking about the expected expressions of that thought at the milestones of adolescence and high school. Those times made no lasting impact on me. The one I do remember was much more unexpected.

The matter at hand was just an ordinary event in life. I was married just a few years. I had just started preaching in Mississippi. All three of my kids were born and were still quite young. My role as a husband and father was still fairly new to me. I awoke one Sunday morning to a vehicle that would not run. The engine in our mini-van had died. How that happened is irrelevant and telling you might ruin any credibility that I have. Suffice it to say it does not often go as low as nine degrees in Mississippi. Whatever the cause, I did what any adult would do. I came up with the $3,100 it cost to have a new engine installed and got the van fixed. The crisis seemed like nothing. It was just a normal financial pinch that happens in life.

This event was different in one way from the emergencies that had occurred before then. I never called my dad for his advice or assistance about it. Several days after the problem had been solved, we spoke on the phone. We talked about what had happened. He did not use the words, "You're a man now, son." There was nothing so melodramatic as that. There was a simple comment made in passing that I had done exactly what he would have.

There was a confidence in his words. His work of training and maturing was bearing the intended fruit. His goal all along was to raise a son that would handle the crises of life just as he would. Every good father wants to transfer his values to his son. He wants to see his son carry on all the good that is in him. There is no greater joy for a father than seeing your son become the kind of man that all of your years of love, guidance, and training intended him to be.

Once that happens, the relationship changes. The thought of my father's disciplining me has not entered my mind – well, I do not remember the last time I feared that. He is still my father. He still owns and deserves my respect and reverence. Yet, there is an intimacy that we can share now that could not possibly exist while I was just his son.

A son serves out of love. He serves to honor his father. I still love my father. I still want to honor him and his life. But that is no longer the only reason I live the way I do. I live the way I do because it seems right to me. I believe that the choices I make are the best choices for my family and me. They happen to be the choices that bring honor to my father, yes. However, I own them now. If my father were removed from the equation of my life, I would still make the same choices that I do now. Where I once served in his house as a son seeking to honor, I now serve as a companion, a fellow-soldier on the same field of battle. My choice is to serve alongside him as a friend.

A Friend of God

The same harmony of motivations and values is required between us and God if we are to become His friend. As difficult as true friendship is between two human souls, it is of little surprise that the sentiment is expressed so infrequently in the Bible. Being called a "friend of God" is one of the rarest descriptions that a man ever receives. Only three times is the phrase found and each of them point to the same man.

In 2 Chronicles 20:7, Jehoshaphat, king of Judah, is preparing for battle against Moab and Ammon. The righteous king turns to God in prayer. In his plea to God, he invokes the name of Abraham and calls him God's friend: "Did you not, our God, drive out the inhabitants of this land before your people Israel, and give it forever to the descendants of Abraham your friend?"

Isaiah, in assuring Israel of God's continuing love of the nation, uses this phrase in reference to Abraham:

> But you, Israel, my servant, Jacob, whom I have chosen, the offspring of Abraham, my friend; you whom I took from the ends of the earth, and called from its farthest corners, saying to you, "You are my servant, I have chosen you and not cast you off"; fear not, for I am with you; be not dismayed, for I am your God; I will strengthen you, I will help you, I will uphold you with my righteous right hand." (Isaiah 41:8-10)

And James in speaking of the connection between faith and works echoed the sentiment in James 2:21-23:

> Was not Abraham our father justified by works when he offered up his son Isaac on the altar? You see that faith was active along with his works, and faith was completed by his works; and the Scripture was fulfilled that says, "Abraham believed God, and it was counted to him as righteousness"- and he was called a friend of God.

One man, three times is called God's friend. That is all. The term's scarcity is probably why as I began the study that lead to this book that "friendship" was not a term that immediately sprang to mind to describe my relationship with God.

Servant, steward, and son are common thoughts in the Bible and are more or less familiar to us. We speak of ourselves in all of those terms as we approach God. As we serve others, we give the glory to God by saying that we are doing that good deed as His servant. When we pray, we make our pleas to Him as His sons. The terms fill our expressions of faith.

But friend? When, if ever, was the last time you called yourself the friend of God? Using that language is too prideful. To us, friendship evokes images of equality and we fall helplessly short of that with God. The images and familiarity we have with friendship are just too common to use to speak of God. No, not friend – we just do not think like that. Nevertheless, there it is, in crisp, black type right in my Bible. Abraham was God's friend.

His walk of fellowship with God is the same walk we are invited to take. We have the privilege of walking not just under the hand of His sovereignty, but to walk at His side holding His hand in companionship. We can know, instinctively, that God is our companion on each step and fellow-soldier in each of life's battles. His presence can add peace in the face of our own weaknesses. The fear of punishment that burdens the lives of servants is lost in our distant past. We are free and even challenged to dream of greater spiritual victories, once we know that we no longer have to win our Father's approval. Knowing God as our friend opens all of Heaven's blessings to our souls.

Abraham's example is even more powerful than that. The texts we just read together do not say that God was Abraham's friend. That might simply suggest devotion and affection from Abraham to God. The Bible says that *Abraham was God's friend*. God calls Abraham "my friend" in Isaiah. He was God's companion. God's great man of faith had become someone whose company God held dear. That is exactly the meaning of "friendship." The New Testament word for friend is "philos." It is defined as meaning "beloved" or "dear" (Arndt and Gingrich 868). Abraham was dear and beloved by God. He was God's friend.

Being God's friend is the example that his life left for us. The connections go beyond just God's becoming dear to us. We understand that concept with very little trouble. God has provided so much for us, culminating in the offering of His Son for us. When someone has given so freely, having an affection for them is easy. No, the example of Abraham is that we can become dear to God. Becoming God's friend means that He holds your company, your fellowship with Him, as something that enriches His existence. If you go back and read those passages in which Abraham is called God's friend, God was acting in the ways that He did because He had affection and respect for His friend. God loved, trusted and treasured His friend. We have been called into that same kind of relationship with God.

Is it possible? Can we really be God's friends? I know it was possible for Abraham, but he was a great man of faith. How can our lives ever hope to measure up to the standard his life has placed before us? I believe it is possible, but in order to understand how we can follow that example, we must first understand what ties our life to Abraham's life. We must understand the strength of the bond we share with him as his spiritual seed.

The Seed of Abraham

When we consider Noah, Abraham, Joseph, Moses, Deborah, David, Elijah, Peter, Paul, and all of the other great men and women of faith, they fill our minds with images of supreme devotion to God. Their lives are surreal to us. The great challenges they faced and the visions given to them by God seem out of reach in our lives of comparative drudgery. They conquered nations, prophesied before kings, and led revivals of God's people. We struggle to meet deadlines at work, get the kids to baseball practice, and clip coupons to save a few dollars at Target. Walking in their steps seems almost unimaginable.

Yet the Bible is emphatic that we do share with them a common existence. In writing about the power of a righteous man's prayer, James uses Elijah as an example. During the days of king Ahab of Israel and his evil Queen Jezebel, Elijah prayed that the rain would stop in Israel (1 Kings 17). For the next 42 months, no rain fell in the nation. His request is a powerful prayer. Surely, having a prayer to stop the rain answered must take some unreachable level of spirituality. True, Elijah was a man of the strongest measure of faith, but that is not the point made by James. Instead he uses Elijah's humanity to assure his readers that their prayers are heard just like the great prophet's. James says, "Elijah was a man with a nature like ours, and he prayed fervently that it might not rain, and for three years and six months it did not rain on the earth" (5:17).

Elijah had a "nature like ours." There is the connection. Prayer is not a blessing reserved only for the man of God who was called to the highest mission of his age, or the prophet or the priest. Answered prayer is a blessing for men of common passions. We can stand on the same spiritual high ground as the greatest of God's servants.

This point is made no more clearly in the Bible than in the case with Abraham. Aside from Jesus, no one figure is more central to the Bible than Abraham. So powerful is his life that human history has been shaped and continues to be shaped by his influence. All of Christendom, Judaism and Islam look back to Abraham as their point of origin (Discussing the validity of those claims is not our aim). The promise given to him by God in Genesis 12 is the central point of the Old Testament. To say that the rest of the Bible is God's description of how He was fulfilling that great promise is no overstatement.

> Now the LORD said to Abram, "Go from your country and your kindred and your father's house to the land that I will show you. And I will make of you a great nation, and I will bless you and make your name great, so that you will be a blessing. I will bless those who bless you, and him who dishonors you I will curse, and in you all the families of the earth shall be blessed." (Genesis 12:1-3)

Understanding his life is critical to understanding the Bible, the work of the Christ, and your individual salvation. We are tied to Abraham. A Christian's faith is following the legacy of faith found in Abraham. Paul's argument to bring Jewish Christians and Gentile Christians together in the churches of Galatia focused on this tie we have in Abraham, "And if you are Christ's, then you are Abraham's offspring, heirs according to promise" (Galatians 3:29). To be in Christ is to be a part of Abraham's family. We are his seed, his spiritual offspring.

His powerful life brings us back to our dilemma again. Abraham's faith is that of a spiritual giant. What possible connection could our lives have to a man like him?

To resolve that perplexity, we must turn back again to the idea of sonship. Biblically, and especially to the Jewish mind, to be called someone's son was to be made equal to that person. That is why the leaders of the Jews in Jesus' day were so incensed that Jesus would call himself the son of God. Look at their reaction to that claim by Jesus in John 5:17-18:

> But Jesus answered them, "My Father is working until now, and I am working." This was why the Jews were seeking all the more to kill him, because not only was he breaking the Sabbath, *but he was even calling God his own Father, making himself equal with God.*

Jesus called God His Father and so He would be God's Son. The Jews took that sentiment to mean equality. A father and son share the same nature. They have the same attributes and abilities. Fathers and sons are equal in person and potential.

Every family member shares a common genetic tie with his parents. Through faith we become the children of Abraham (Galatians 3:7). As such, we share a common spiritual nature with Abraham. That shared genetic tie in the family of God is faith. It is the mutual spiritual cord that binds each of God's people together. From Abel to Samuel and the prophets in Hebrews 11, faith is the foundation of all of their lives.

Abraham is the archetype of that faith. God's description of this man is that he is the "father of all who believe" (Romans 4:11). God looked over His creation and pointed to one man as the example of faith: Abraham. The other heroes of God found in the Bible had great faith, but Abraham's faith is unique in one way. The great promise given to him in Genesis 12 meant that he would hold a place that no other man could. His example of faith in following his call would serve to show the Israelites how to live with God for 1,500 years. His faith gives all Christians that same hope today. There is a faith that saves. Better still, there is a faith that brings me to the height of intimacy with God. So as much as any human could, Abraham epitomized what God wants from each of us.

In terms of faith, we have just seen that we are Abraham's sons. What does that mean? Our sonship to Abraham means that we share in a faith that has the same nature, attributes and abilities as his. Our faith is equal in its potential to that of Abraham. That is exactly Paul's point as he examines the faith of Abraham in Romans 4. His aim is to show that the blessings of Abraham's faith are open for every person in the world. His argument is that any man who comes to God in faith can stand where Abraham stood. We share in the power of Abraham's faith:

> That is why it depends on faith, in order that the promise may rest on grace and be guaranteed to all his offspring--not only to the adherent of the law but also *to the one who shares the faith of Abraham, who is the father of us all,* as it is written, "I have made you the father of many nations" – in the presence of the God in whom he believed, who gives life to the dead and calls into existence the things that do not exist. (Romans 4:16-17)

We are the offspring of the man who was called the "friend of God." His faith is our faith. His walk with God can and should be ours. Our father was the friend of God. Because of our familial tie to Abraham, the question we should be asking is not, "How can I be like Abraham?" The question of our hearts should be, "Why am I not like my father, Abraham, now?"

The example of Abraham's life lays out the blueprint for us to follow to become like him in friendship with God. The defining quality of Abraham's life is his faith in God. Whether in leaving Ur or yielding the Promised Land to Lot or in waiting for and offering his son, Isaac, his trust in God never wavered. That faith or trust carried him across the ancient world and brought him into his friendship with God. So it is, in looking at his life, that we can see the primary principle of friendship with God. If faith defines Abraham, and Abraham epitomizes friendship with God, then there is a necessary tie between faith and friendship that we must explore and understand.

Faith – the Path to Friendship

I believe that principle can be stated simply by saying, "*Faith fulfilled ends in friendship.*" The power of faith to lead us to friendship is inherent within faith itself. Faith's potency is not determined by the person who holds it. God does not honor a person's circumstances, heritage, intellect or any of the other attributes so highly valued in our world. He values faith. Faith transforms the soul. Every person in whom faith is

32

found will be changed. The end of that trusting submission to the love, guidance, and discipline of God turns servants to stewards and stewards to sons. Finally, faith grows sons into friends.

I know that is how it happened in my life. Under the hand of a loving father, my life was ordered and compelled to follow a fixed set of values. He required of me honesty, morality, and integrity. As a child, I feared his wrath. In time, I began to trust in his love for me. I knew that his rules were there for my own good. They were an expression of his love. As that trust or faith in his goodness matured within me, they began to define me. His goodness toward me, created faith in my heart toward him. That faith transformed my soul to be like his. All of his work in raising his son was aimed toward making that son his friend.

Once the son has been made like his father, the relationship is forever changed. No longer does he see in his father an autocrat. The fear of the father's judgment fades from his memory. His father is no longer a disciplinarian. He is a counselor and companion. The distance between the two disappears. There is a trust and openness that has never been known before. The son and the father are one. They are one in mind and spirit. True fellowship exists. The father's constant, guiding love and the son's faith in his father has made them friends.

The transformation is no different for a child of God. Faith has led him to follow God's direction. He has lived in God's house and been trained in God's ways. When once his thoughts were not God's thoughts and his ways not God's ways, that now has changed. He sees the world as God sees it and sees sin as God sees it. The son has grown into the image of His Father. Faith has transformed him.

The step from sonship to friendship is natural. A son that never becomes an adult is unnatural. The son that never leaves home, starts his own family, and grows his own career is a source of shame to his father. A grown man living still in his father's house is unhealthy in his development. At some point, this natural progression of growth results in his becoming like his father. He will do on his own the things he has been brought up to do.

The step into friendship can also be difficult. Inexperience with the new dynamics of the relationship can be uncomfortable. Do you remember the first time you picked up the check after a meal with your parents? How did the first Thanksgiving dinner at your house instead of theirs go? The adjustments can be hard. Insecurities in either the father or son can also make the transition complicated. Sharing your thoughts, fears, and needs with someone whose diapers you have changed or who has changed yours can be threatening. Growing the relationship takes time and effort.

No matter how difficult, the process does produce a wonderful result. The communion that grows throughout the son's maturation is what every good father wants for his son. Our children can never be too mature. Yes, we can get uncomfortable in seeing our children grow up "too fast." However. our discomfort is just one of the insecurities we just mentioned. No matter his age, seeing your son make wise and spiritually sound choices is never a disappointment. A good father stands ready to give his son the room to grow into manhood, as the son is ready.

Only a selfish and manipulative father would stand in the way of that growth. God is neither of those things. He is the perfect example of a Father. All of His guidance in our lives is pointing us to be transformed into sons who are like Him. Our growth, our maturation takes nothing away from His glory. He never wants our growth to stop. There is never a time that He will prevent our intimacy from deepening. He has no limit on the intimacy of communion expressed in James 4:8, "Draw near to God, and he will draw near to you." At what point would God say, "Stop, you've grown too much, too fast. You have drawn too near. Back up."? There is none.

All of God's work in your life is calling you into this relationship. God's work in this world depends on all who wear His name to seize the opportunities that surround them. What kind of people do you suppose God wants representing Him in this world? His servants will do all that they are told (Luke 17:10), but will they do more? His stewards will use only the treasure for which they are responsible. Even sons may stop their service once they feel the Father is honored. Friends will never stop working. Their service is not externally motivated by punishment, reward or praise. Their service is natural and instinctive. Friends of God never have to ask, "What would Jesus do?" They already know. Their fulfilled faith has made them God's friends. Faith has transformed them.

Faith fulfilled ends in friendship. At least one man in scripture lived with that kind of faith. The model of our faith grew into an unrestrained fellowship with God. Abraham's example beckons us to

34

follow. His example is one of unity, trust, and sharing. He leads us to a life where we commune with God even as we labor in His service; in which the fear of His judgment has faded from our memory; where we honor Him not out of duty, but out of the expression of a common spirit. His work becomes our work. His ways are our ways. We can conceive of no other life. If one could remove God from the equation of our lives, we would not change. We would live the same life as we did previously because we own the moral and spiritual values we follow. Faith has transformed us to be like our Father.

You must believe that a relationship of friendship is God's goal for your life. God's word is full of exhortations for His people to grow. There is not one command to stop. Remaining as a servant in God's house is unnatural. He wants His servants to grow in their works:

> Now in a great house there are not only vessels of gold and silver but also of wood and clay, some for honorable use, some for dishonorable. Therefore, if anyone cleanses himself from what is dishonorable, he will be a vessel for honorable use, set apart as holy, useful to the master of the house, ready for every good work. (2 Timothy 2:20-21)

He wants His servants to grow. Remaining just a son in God's house is unnatural. He wants the same growth for His children, "Like newborn infants, long for the pure spiritual milk, that by it you may grow up into salvation" (1 Peter 2:2).

Within the nature of faith is the power to create friends with God. Your faith, like Abraham's faith, has that seed of friendship with God within it. Your growth from servant to son and from son to friend is natural, expected, and desired by God. Abraham's faith preaches that message. I can be God's friend because of the inherent nature and power of faith and not because of some special ability within me or special measure of faith granted to me. The same is true of the faith within your heart. All faith, if allowed to grow without restraint, draws man closer to God and into a communion that the Bible calls "friendship."

So ask yourself now: Are you walking down the path of friendship with God that Abraham has highlighted for us? You have joined Abraham by having faith in God. Just as Abraham did long ago, you have given your life over to God's service. However, if you share in Abraham's faith, why do you not share in his blessings?

Let me ask it another way. I would guess you would like to be closer to God. Most Christians I know would say, 'Yes' without hesitation. Well, if you would like to be closer to Him, then what is it that is holding you back?

God is not the obstacle. He is a good Father, the perfect Father. He has done and will do everything needed to open the way into His heart. God has cleared every hurdle on His part to allow us to find friendship with Him. He will never stop or hinder your growth. There is nothing more He needs to do or to change to be your Friend.

We are our only obstacle. Our inability to accept that God would desire our meager affections toward Him stops us from conceiving of ourselves as His friends. The progress of our faith stops when our faith can no longer see how to draw any nearer to Him. The limitations of our own faith are all that stand between God and us. If faith fulfilled ends in friendship and you are unable to see how you can be His friend, then your faith has not yet been fulfilled.

God has provided the blessings of friendship to us. The nature of the friendship is life-changing. We need to understand this friendship. We need to understand that the trusting submission of faith will bring us to the door of that great blessing.

The journey that Abraham took from Ur to Mt. Moriah is the model we have to help us understand how we can grow into the friendship with God that He has opened to us. Child of God, the step from son to friend awaits you. Let's walk together in the footsteps of the faith of Abraham as He leaves Ur behind and takes the first steps of friendship with God. There is a great treasure that awaits discovery along the journey.

PART 2 - I AM GOD'S SERVANT

Our walk with God begins as servants. When the Prodigal Son returned to his father, he felt himself so unworthy that his mind could envision himself as nothing more than a servant in a master's house.

But when he came to himself, he said, "How many of my father's hired servants have more than enough bread, but I perish here with hunger! I will arise and go to my father, and I will say to him, 'Father, I have sinned against Heaven and before you. I am no longer worthy to be called your son. Treat me as one of your hired servants.'" (Luke 15:17-19)

The touch of sin and failure in our lives humbles us. In the poverty of spirit that we share with the Prodigal, we are brought to God. Realizing our short-comings also limits our imagination about what is possible in our relationship with Him. Being poor in spirit leaves us recognizing our need for growth and improvement. The lingering touch of our neediness before God is why most people begin walking with Him thinking about reward and punishment. That metric is both powerful enough to keep us faithful to God and rigid enough to keep God's true nature isolated from our hearts. This is a stage of faith we need to experience, never need to forget, but must grow beyond to see all that God has given to us.

In Part 2, we will join Abraham as he is learning the lessons of being a servant and a steward. Abraham is already growing toward God when we are introduced to him. Yet, the basis of his relationship in Genesis 12 and 13 is still one of reward and punishment. As God deals with Abraham, the promise is, "Go from your country . . . and I will make you" and then "Lift up your eyes . . . I will give to you" (Genesis 12:1-2; 13:14-15). He needed to learn the lessons of servanthood before he could move closer to God. So must we.

3

OUT OF UR
"ACCEPTING THE JOURNEY"
(GENESIS 11:27-12:4)

"Do two walk together, unless they have agreed to meet?
(Amos 3:3)

His name is Jimmy. Well, he is "Jim" now. He grew up in the same church as my wife. I met him at the same time that I met Julie. From 9 years of age all the way through high-school, the three of us were always together.

Jimmy was a close friend to both my wife and me. They shared their first kiss together. Ok, they were only four years old at the time, but I still count it and will not let him forget it. Jimmy and I spent countless hours in each other's homes over the years. We did all of the things together that adolescents and teenagers do. The night he shot me in the head with a BB gun cemented our relationship in a way that only makes sense to young boys. Yes, the man who kissed my wife and shot me with a gun was one of my dearest friends.

Then we left high school. The chubby-cheeked kid we used to call "Pillsbury Doughboy" had grown into a massive young man. He went

39

to the University of Louisville on a football scholarship to play for Howard Schnellenberger. He started for them as a defensive tackle. Julie and I went off to a small private school named Freed-Hardeman University.

The three of us stayed in touch for a while. We went to see Louisville play against Memphis State one year. In time, Jimmy made it to the NFL for a season. He played for the New Orleans Saints. Julie and I made it down for a Monday night game against the Dallas Cowboys.

Over the years, the visits faded away. We saw him once when a mutual friend hosted a reunion of sorts. I called him after Katrina hit New Orleans where he was then living. We spoke again after the death of Julie's mother. Our last visit with him occurred a couple of years ago on a trip that took Julie and me through Louisiana. We have not spent any meaningful time together in many years. Still, every time we talk, the conversation is easy. There was nothing that ever drove us apart. Our paths simply diverged. We stopped walking down the same road. He took one fork. Julie and I took another.

We still hold Jimmy as a friend and I am confident he does the same for us, but the relationship has not grown in years. Our choices led us in different walks of life. When our paths diverged, our interaction ended. Without being involved in each other's lives there is no hope of that friendship ever getting stronger.

I imagine no one has poked Jimmy in the stomach while saying "Pillsbury" in a long time, but Julie could do it and we would all laugh at the memory. The nickname given to Jimmy as a boy does not fit Jim, the man. I do not know the nickname that fits now. We do not know each other like that anymore.

Old Friends

There is a reason we use the expression, "like talking to an old friend." When you reunite with someone from your past, the conversation often picks up right where it left off. You resurrect the conversations that are buried in your past. You have to because the relationship stopped progressing when you parted ways. The old connections are all that are left. A relationship can grow only as long as each person agrees about its path. Even when two people are compatible, without agreement on the path that they should walk the relationship will reach a plateau.

The need for constant interaction in friendship is an important concept to understand in our relationship with God. To find friendship with God we have to walk as far down the path with Him as we can. When our spirits turn aside or even pause in our walk with Him, we can grow no closer to Him. Our hesitancy puts distance between Him and us because His work is never done and He never stops walking. That distance may not stop us from serving Him, but it will keep us from knowing Him. By staying where we are, we will never become His friends.

Staying in Ur

Abraham's introduction in the Bible occurs when God appears to him in Genesis 12 and calls him to leave his home, Ur, and his family behind. His obedience to that call led him on an amazing journey of growth and faith with God. However, I want you to imagine for a moment that Abraham never left Ur. For some reason that we do not know, he could not bring himself to leave his home. Could Abraham have served God faithfully in his Chaldean home? He would be in need of forgiveness for disobedience for not leaving, true, but that is not our point. Just assume that Abraham stayed and that he repented. He implored God for forgiveness in whatever way was appropriate in Abraham's day. God, being a gracious God, would have restored Abraham, but He would have already selected another to carry out His plan. Abraham's chance to leave Ur and go on that incredible walk with God would have been gone.

What then for Abraham? He certainly could have renewed his walk with God. He could have gone on to use his life as a beacon in Ur pointing people to God. Abraham would have had a good existence. His influence may have changed Ur for the better. He may have never missed what might have been.

"The Good" vs. "The Best"

Staying in Ur may have turned out for the "good," but it would never be what was "best." He would have never been called the "Friend of God." He would have never been the "Father of all who believe." No matter the cause, be it sinfulness or simple weakness, if Abraham had chosen not to walk with God out of Ur, his life would have been less full than it could have been.

Our call to walk with God does not have the same prophetic sharpness as Abraham's but the qualities governing it are identical. Every day our faith is challenged to take another step with God. Some days those challenges are as simple as making a choice to utter a word in His name to a friend or stranger. Some days those challenges shake the very foundations of faith with their severity. Small to the point of almost being missed or so large as to be life changing, the tests all require the same from us. They require our faith to take one more step with God.

Every time we take that step, we move toward "the best." Every obstacle placed before us by faith is a call to be more than we are. We are being beckoned to become like our Father. The growth of our faith is inviting us to friendship.

When we pause or fail to take that step, we have not thrown off God. More often, we have chosen the good instead of the best. We have chosen to serve God in the place where we are instead of seeking to be more like Him. The choice does not necessitate that we have become unfaithful. We just have more room to grow. We are still looking at ourselves as His servants, stewards or maybe sons. We are just not ready to be His friends. Friendship comes when faith is fulfilled. Faith is fulfilled when it responds instinctively just as God would when a challenge is placed before it. God always faces the obstacles in front of Him. The more naturally we do the same, the closer we are to sharing His nature and fulfilling our faith.

The path to faith's fulfillment starts with agreement. We will make that choice when we see things as God sees them. Most often, we make it even before we can comprehend where it will take us. To find friendship with God, we must agree that no matter the challenge, our spirits will always walk together with Him.

Abraham chose agreement with God. He was called out of Ur by God and he followed. The first step he took away from his home was a step of agreement. Abraham knew that God was right. For Abraham to take his family on this journey meant that God was right that Ur should be left behind. He agreed with God that he was the right man to come out of Ur. Abraham agreed with God that something better than Ur was waiting.

In these ways our lives need to mimic Abraham's. There are some essential areas of life about which we must be in agreement with God in order to walk with Him. We must agree with Him in His assessment of the world, His assessment of ourselves, and His plan for us. Not until we grow in all of these areas can our faith move to find its fulfillment of friendship with God.

Agreeing About the World

Ur was a city-state of the Sumerians. The Sumerian people were renowned for their innovations and culture. They created their pictographic writing, cuneiform, around the same time as the Egyptians created their hieroglyphics. They were the first people to adopt the method of numbering time in 60 unit blocks. Our earliest known laws come from their land (Pfeiffer, "Bible Atlas" 47). Their people were well-educated in the sciences and highly literate (Free 46).

In the city of Ur, an average, middle-class family lived in a home of 10-20 rooms with plastered walls. The house itself would have measured about 40 feet x 50 feet (qtd. in Free 46). While it is difficult to know the exact conditions of Ur when Abraham lived in it, he was part of a city and culture that rivaled any in the world and surpassed most. He lived in the New York or Paris of his day.

Nevertheless, Ur had its downside, which is not to be missed. It was a city separated from God. Archaeologists have found evidence that the servants of kings and queens were killed and buried with their ruler at the ruler's death (Pfieffer, "History" 54). Idolatry was rampant in the city. The Bible even comments on the worship of false gods and the impact upon Abraham's family:

And Joshua said to all the people, "Thus says the LORD, the God of Israel, 'Long ago, your fathers lived beyond the Euphrates, *Terah, the father of Abraham and of Nahor*; and they served other gods Then I took your father Abraham from beyond the River and led him through all the land of Canaan, and made his offspring many. I gave him Isaac.' . . . . And if it is evil in your eyes to serve the LORD, choose this day whom you will serve, *whether the gods your fathers served in the region beyond the River*, or the gods of the Amorites in whose land you dwell.

But as for me and my house, we will serve the LORD." (Joshua 24:2-3, 15)

Whether Abraham ever served idols is not specified. We do know that his family did and that the people in Ur had many of them.

Abraham Agreed About Ur

Abraham heard God's call and left Ur, never questioning why he should leave the sophisticated city. His eyes saw Ur as God saw Ur. Abraham was not blinded by the riches that international trade had brought to it. He was not satisfied with the bounty that the Sumerian's mastery of irrigation had placed on his table. He could see Ur as something that could be left behind.

His journey out of the city was more than just obedience to God; it was agreement with Him. The writer of Hebrews tells us as much when he says, "If they had been thinking of that land from which they had gone out, they would have had opportunity to return" (Hebrews 11:15). Abraham never deemed his home a place to return. He must have seen it as it was. Ur was a place of physical prestige. Abraham, like God, was focused on the spiritual.

Abraham Hesitates to Leave Family

Abraham was called to leave more than just his country. The call he received said, "Go from your country and your kindred and your father's house to the land that I will show you" (Genesis 12:1). God said, leave your country, your relatives, and your father. Abraham appears to have done the first part immediately, but to hesitate on the rest.

The Bible appears to list two calls for Abraham to leave. Acts 7 makes it clear that the original call came to Abraham in Ur before he moved to Haran (Acts 7:2). In the Bible's text, the call of Genesis 12 comes after he moves from Ur to Haran. In fact, the move to Haran is credited not to Abraham, but to Terah, Abraham's father:

Terah took Abram his son and Lot the son of Haran, his grandson, and Sarai his daughter-in-law, his son Abram's wife, and they went forth together from Ur of the Chaldeans to go into the land of Canaan, but when they came to Haran, they settled there. (Genesis 11:31)

Not until the death of Terah does Abraham move from Haran to the Promised Land (Genesis 11:32; 12:4-5).

Commentators are divided as to whether Genesis 12:1-3 is a distinct call given to Abraham after the death of Terah or just the statement of the call recorded in Acts 7. For our purposes, the number of and timing of calls does not matter.

Haran was never Abraham's final destination. Terah was never invited to join his son in the Promised Land. No one knows why Abraham moved to Haran and stopped there with Terah. God never voices any displeasure that Abraham remained there until Terah's death. Again, the reason for his delay does not matter.

What matters is that Abraham is not prepared to walk with God into the Promised Land until he is ready to complete God's call to leave country *and* father. Either God cannot show Abraham the Promised Land, or Abraham is not ready to see that land, until his father is gone. There is no way around the fact that Abraham's faith needed to grow further before he could move on from Haran. Until he saw that the greater good for his life was leaving his family behind and heading to Canaan, God could not use him fully. He could go only as far as his agreement with God would allow.

Do We See What God Sees?

We face the same challenges. Our walk with God goes only as far as we see that it needs to go. If we view the world as a lovely home in which we live with all the comforts of life, we are in no hurry to leave it. However, if we see this world as a home being engulfed in the flames of a raging fire, we have no choice but to run from it and so to run into God's arms. To grow toward friendship with God, we must see the world as he sees it.

However, just as Abraham, we often have attachments in this life that seem too dear to release. Abraham hesitated with his family in Haran. His delay does not appear to be considered sinful by God, but it did limit Abraham's growth for a time. Family ties often cause that delay with us as do many other things. Be it career ambitions or pleasure-seeking activities or whatever holds our attention, these pursuits can halt our spiritual growth.

We are not talking here about actions that are inherently sinful. Our scope is not the sinful. Sinful things do not just impact our spiritual development, they can destroy it altogether. Our focus is on the areas of life that are natural and even wholesome.

No man can be faulted for being a lover of his family or having a strong work ethic and desire to be productive in his career. However, those things can be so encompassing to the affections of our hearts that we can lose sight of the higher calling that is beckoning us for more. God's view of those things is always spiritual. He always sees them from the standpoint of eternity. We should, too.

You are What You Eat

Think of it this way. Your family budget has a set amount in it for food. When you walk into the grocery store and start buying food, every dollar you have can only be spent once. Each choice you make excludes some other food item from being purchased. So when you buy the candy bar or soft drink, you cannot buy as many fruits or vegetables as you could otherwise. Your choice is not wrong. The money you have is yours. You can buy whatever you want in the store with your money. Nevertheless, your choice does have consequences. By choosing to buy foods on the basis of preference and not nutrition, you have limited the amount of nutrition your family receives.

Over time, those choices can impact your physical health. You may not have the energy or stamina you would like. You may gain weight and become dissatisfied with your appearance. Without ever doing anything overtly wrong, you have impacted your body in ways that limit your enjoyment of life.

The same is true spiritually. We are finite beings and the budget of our lives' resources is limited. We only have so much time and energy to spend in this world. Every time we make a choice to expend our resources, it limits the amount we can spend elsewhere. Our lives get so full so fast. I doubt there is much time in your life right now that is not already claimed by something.

Over time, that fullness has an impact. We wake up one morning to an emptiness in the soul we were not expecting. Our spirits are crying out to be fed. They are starving for something that truly nourishes them. But we have already spent all of our "money" on junk food. Many of the activities of our busy lives give little of substance to our spirit.

Why do we not do better or at least do differently? Perhaps, the choices are harder than we want to make.

Could We Leave Ur?

That is really the issue. We cannot walk with God on this journey of friendship until we are ready to leave Ur. The good cannot be exchanged for the best without leaving the good behind. Growing means there are hard choices in front of us.

Staying in Ur would have been easy for Abraham. He would have been comfortable there. From all evidence, it would have been a wonderful existence. He could have served God in peace in a place of relative ease. The people of his city would have seen in him the kind of person they would want to be one day. His influence would have turned some of the idolaters in his home back to the one true God. Abraham's life would have benefitted an entire city for God but his choice was to leave and by joining God on that journey, he left the good for others and took the best. His life did not just change a city, it changed the world and eternity.

Leaving the good is never easy. Making that choice is a challenge every time. You are already a spiritual person. Your life is already filled with good, but the fact that you are still reading suggests that you want more. You want the best. There is only one way. You have to leave the good behind.

What is your "Ur?" What is the good in your life? This discussion is a call to self-reflection – honest self-reflection. If we were talking about leaving the "evil" for the good, the line of demarcation would be clear. We are not. For the kind of person likely reading this book, evil is not the hindrance. Your greatest obstacle in your life is the good. Your industriousness is good. You must care for your family. Your place is to be involved in your children's lives, your community, and your school. Every Christian should be busy in the work of his church. The question is, "Are those things the best?"

How many times in your life have you ever had a dream about doing something more with God? I would guess countless. Many men think of preaching, only to pull back before doing it. Countless consider doing mission work or trading a corporate life for a life of beneficent service to others, only to let the impulse of a dream fade. So many dreams of the best die to the necessity of the good.

Faith always moves toward the best. Within your spirit is the dream to reach the best. The challenge is that it is unreachable until you give up the good. There is comfort and familiarity with the good. I only know of one motivation to let go and seek for the best. That motivation is faith that God walks with you from the good to the best. Fear says, "The good is all there is" or "The best cannot be found." Fear causes us to doubt that more can be found. The doubt stops us in our growth toward God. Faith says, "I know God knows the best and will lead me to find it." Faith moves to the best.

God could not use Abraham fully in Ur. He could not use him fully in Haran. He needed Abraham in Canaan. God needs you to trust that it is ok to leave the good behind. The walk from the good to the best is the walk of faith. Leaving the good behind is the walk of friendship. God needs you to join Him in Canaan.

Agreeing About Yourself

Here is another list of Bible characters. What do they have in common: Moses, Gideon, Solomon, Isaiah, and Jeremiah?

They have at least two points of commonality. All five were called by God and all five first responded with reluctance at the call. Even in their reluctance, there is a common thread:

- Moses complained, "Who am I that I should go to Pharaoh?" (Exodus 3:10).
- Gideon offered, "[H]ow can I save Israel . . . I am least in my father's house" (Judges 6:15).
- Solomon said, "I am but a child" (1 Kings 3:7).
- Isaiah confessed, "I am lost; for I am a man of unclean lips" (Isaiah 6:5).
- Jeremiah echoed the same feelings as he said, "I am only a youth" (Jeremiah 1:6).

48

Each one of these great men was faced with a call toward the best. When confronted with that great challenge, each was forced to look inward and confess his own inabilities to accomplish what God was asking.

How could they respond in any other way? No man should think himself qualified to provide deliverance for God's people as Moses and Gideon did. No man should claim in himself the wisdom to rule over or prophesy to His people. In fact, any man who is comfortable taking those roles upon himself is likely the very one that should not assume them. All of these men of God were called to the best, and that encounter crystallized for them their own weaknesses.

Yet God still called them. Did God not know about Moses' failures in life? Was He unaware of Isaiah's sin or Jeremiah's youth? Was God wrong in selecting these men to do the job He needed done? No, God is never wrong. Each of these men was exactly the man that God needed to accomplish His will. He uses men who are "poor in spirit." His work is not done by the proud but by the humble. God uses men in their weakness, not their strength:

> His delight is not in the strength of the horse, nor his pleasure in the legs of a man, but the LORD takes pleasure in those who fear him, in those who hope in his steadfast love. (Psalm 147:10-11)

God shaped His plan to use these men. They were ideally suited to do just what God needed. God knew these men. He knew their strengths and weaknesses. He knew they could carry out the role for which they had been selected.

Abraham Agreed About Abraham

This principle was also true in the life of Abraham. God's testimony of him was, "For I know him, that he will command his children and his household after him, and they shall keep the way of the LORD" (Genesis 18:19).

"I know him," God said. In other words, "He is the right man for the job." In God's perfect wisdom, He surveyed the whole world and found the right person to call to Canaan. God never makes a mistake. When He called Abraham, He called the right man.

The call to leave Ur was about more than the condition of Ur. The call was also about the character of Abraham. If Abraham believed himself to be too small, too weak, or too frail for God to use, he would have never left. Fear and doubt would have told Abraham that he was not worthy of the blessing. Those insecurities would have said that his dream of seeing that heavenly city was too grand and too bold for him. Self-loathing would have paralyzed his steps and kept him in Ur. His journey out of Ur was a journey of faith in himself. The foundation of that faith was created in the call. The God, who knew him best said, "Come." God gave witness to His belief in Abraham's faith. He knew Abraham could reach Canaan and become our father of faith. If that were not possible, He would have never called Abraham.

The only thing in doubt is whether or not Abraham would agree with God's choice. Abraham had to know that God would not lead him into a place where he could not go. He needed a firm conviction that God would not open a door of opportunity too grand for him to enter. God trusted Abraham to walk with Him. Abraham needed to comprehend how much God believed in the man He was calling.

Get Yourself Ready

"Get yourself ready and God will use you," is another statement I heard many times from my father as I grew as a child of God. The thought voiced his belief in what we are trying to express here. God uses people who are ready to be used. This thought can be seen in the coming of Jesus. Man was not ready to receive the Messiah when Adam and Eve left the garden. He needed seasoning. Humanity needed to understand its own helplessness in sin. Because man first needed seasoning, God sent the Law of Moses to bring man to the Christ. He never asked any man to submit to Jesus until he had prepared mankind to understand what that action would mean. God never asks a person to do more than he can.

God only asks what man can accomplish. Abraham is called out of Ur long before he is asked to offer Isaac in sacrifice. The order is important. There is growth from Ur to Moriah. Three decades of trusting in and learning of God seasoned Abraham to be ready to accept the challenge inherent in God's asking for Isaac's life.

My father's statement conveyed that sentiment. God cannot use you until you are ready to be used. He cannot use a man to preach the gospel until that man prepares his heart and mind to do it. God cannot use an uncompassionate Christian to comfort the grieving. He cannot use a selfish heart to give to those in need.

Nevertheless, the real power in the thought is on the other side. *God will use you.* When my father told me that over and again as I started preaching, he was warning me against something he had seen many young preachers do. It is easy to be caught up in church politics. Many young men have gone too far in trying to be noticed, speak on the biggest lectures, or preach at prestigious churches. Ambition is a part of everyone's character – even preachers. He wanted his son to avoid that desire. There is no need for self-promotion. God will bring you to the place of service which is best for you.

God will use you. There is the key. God will, not God might. Your time of service is coming. Get yourself ready. God knows when you are ready to serve. He knows when there is work to be done. God knows when you are the right man or woman to do the job. Your task is to be ready.

You Are Ready

You do believe that God is working in this world, right? If you believe that, then you are compelled to think that at least some of the opportunities that arise in your life are the result of His influence in this world. Not everything is coincidence or just circumstantial. Some of the events in your life are providential.

Those providential events are the calls of God on your life of which we are speaking. They are your call out of "Ur" and to the best. God's providence is giving His testimony that you are ready to be used. He trusts you to take another step toward friendship. Those events are always blessings, but they are blessings that challenge and frighten us.

The hardest part of finding the best is always internal. External circumstances and obstacles do lie between where we are and where God would have us to be. They are never the barriers that stop us. Those barriers have never stopped God's people when they have stepped forward following His direction. However, inward, spiritual struggles stop God's people every day.

We are hindered by the struggle of agreement about self. Have you ever looked into the eyes of someone struggling with the pains of sin or weeping in grief and felt yourself too small for the challenge? The opportunity stands right there in front of you, but your words seem too insignificant to meet the challenge. "Surely, someone else can help this person," you wishfully whisper to yourself, but there is no one else there. You are the one who went to the hospital. You responded to the need of another without needing to be directed to go. So, there you stand with a soul who needs to see God. Are you ready?

God says you are. He never uses people who are not ready. The only question is whether or not you agree with His choice. The call to speak or to serve is there. God has cast His vote in bringing the opportunity to you. He is saying, "You are ready." You have cast your vote about your readiness by walking to the open door of opportunity. Now, it is time to trust yourself. The opportunity is here because you are ready. Do you believe you are ready?

Immediately, you can think of others who know more, speak better, are more qualified, or have more experience. In that moment, you become Moses or Gideon. Just as those great servants of God did, you find yourself overwhelmed at the thought of taking the next step. You might be right. There are people who might appear more qualified. Yet in spite of appearances, they are not looking into the eyes of your lost friend or holding the hand of that struggling stranger. You are. God who controls the world has you there and no one else.

He is saying, "You are ready." Every time our faith is challenged and called to move forward, His testimony is given. We walk the path to friendship as we meet the challenges to our faith. Until we fulfill that faith, friendship is only a dream.

You are ready.

Agreeing About His Plans

For Abraham, leaving Ur meant he agreed with God about one other thing. He believed the best could be found. Abraham was no cynic. He rejected Solomon's refrain of 500 years later, "All is vanity!"

His faith in God compelled him to leave Ur because he knew that God was calling him into a better place. We have made the point that Abraham agreed that Ur needed to be left behind. The willingness to leave can only occur with this thought attached to it. If staying in Ur is no different than leaving it, why did he leave? Abraham can leave Ur only as he is able to see there is something better out there. He had to agree that going to the "land which God would show him" was better than staying in the land in which he lived. He had to believe that God's plan was the best plan for his life. If he did not, he would have never moved.

"The Best" – God's Plan for You

Your path to friendship really begins with an absolute trust that God both knows what is best for you and is also working to bring the best into your life. If you do not hold that conviction firmly within your mind, you will forever question every opportunity you are given. You will take your walk down the path of cynicism and away from friendship.

The commitment about the goodness of God that we need is not an arbitrary choice. Our confidence comes from the evidence that flows from the testimony of the Bible. Much of the Bible is written to reveal to us the nature of the God we are serving. We are shown His faithfulness to Noah, Abraham, Joseph, and dozens of other people of faith to teach us that He will always be faithful to us. This commitment is also built on experiential evidence. Live with God long enough and you will see that His path for you is always the best one. Take the Golden Rule and use it in your life. Use that great teaching as the banner of your life for one year. Then look back and see if you are not in a better place spiritually. Just see if you have not grown as a person. You will not be able to stop your life and relationships from experiencing spiritual growth. The commitment that begins your path to friendship welcomes you to test it.

With that commitment in hand, the call to Canaan is an inviting one. The opportunity to find more in life than you have ever imagined is yours to seize. I do not know God's plan for your life or for mine in detail. I do know that Jesus called it an "abundant life" (John 10:10). His abundant life is a life full of the best. Faith convicts me that God is walking with me from the good to the best. That is enough for me. Our abundant life is lived out of the good of Ur and in the best of Canaan.

God is calling you to join Him in Canaan. Now, how do you find it?

Finding Canaan – Yours is not Mine

You have never been called into the literal land of Canaan. Only Abraham was. His journey of faith into the Promised Land led to his friendship with God – not yours. You must realize that your journey may not be like someone else's.

That ambiguity may be part of the reason that this concept is so hard to grasp and accept. Our world is driven by productivity. From the first day of school until the last day of our working lives, people are judging our performance. Most of the time, that judgment is made against an established scale and in comparison to our peers. The process of evaluation we endure conditions us to think in those terms.

That metric is rarely a good idea in spiritual terms. Following Abraham to Canaan would not have given you anything special in relation to the spiritual. His journey was his work with God and no one else's. If you had been in Ur when Abraham was, your "Canaan" may very well have been found in Ur. God's work in your life may have reached its fullness without you ever changing your physical location.

Finding "Canaan" may not involve living in a particular place, working in one special field or accomplishing some rigid task. The "Canaan" we seek is the one that allows God to use our lives without restriction. The journey of which we are speaking is the journey Abraham completed as God said of him, "and have not withheld" (Genesis 22:16). He reached the "Canaan" of which we speak not by entering the physical border of a region, but by accepting the fullness of his fellowship with God.

The "Canaan" we are seeking is one of relationship. Yours may not (and likely will not) be mine. What we are suggesting is that friendship with God exists when we do naturally the things that God would do in our place. Given that we are different people and possess different personalities and skills, your walk with God will lead you to a different place than mine. You will end up learning different lessons and sharing different experiences in His service than I do.

These differences are expected by God. He has prepared this world and His church to make use of them. I enjoy the process of teaching, and so I do it. I am much less skilled as a pastor or caregiver. Others are. On our journeys, I can find "Canaan" in teaching, and they can find it as a pastor or hundreds of other ways.

In fact, I would suggest that even our own "Canaan" can change. The first time you exchange the good for the best, all you are really getting is the "better." You have made a change. That action has drawn you closer to God. At that point, you are as close as you have ever been with Him. What if you continue to grow? What once was the best will naturally become the good when something even better appears. And so, you move. You make the decision again to press on in your spiritual walk. Your eyes are opened to see more and to make more of the opportunities surrounding you.

This process keeps on going until doubt or fear stops it. You keep making that exchange until you no longer agree that the "Ur" you are in needs to be left behind or that you have the ability to take the next step to this new and challenging "Canaan" your faith now sees in front of you. That pause or stop in your journey is not necessarily bad. You can live well in Ur and serve God well at the point of life you have now. However, you have stopped short of what could be. For even the most spiritually mature Christian, there is another "Canaan" that awaits. No one has ever exhausted the intimacy that God has to offer. Sooner or later, you will become comfortable with the good.

That means your best is found at that pinnacle of your faith. However close to the heart of God your faith can see is the best. Yours and mine will be different in appearance. They are the same in blessings.

Still, we have not answered the question practically. What do you need to *do* to find your Canaan?

Finding Canaan – Do not Trust the "Prophet"

I have never had a vision from God. I seriously question those today that say they have. The Bible teaches those kind of events are not going on today.

Let us be clear on this point. The prophetic visions and manifestations of God to the men and women of the Bible are no longer occurring. Most of what is called "Christendom" today mocks the Mormon faith for following the claimed prophetic visions of Joseph Smith. However, many of those same people follow, without question, their own pastor's weekly claim that God has laid some special message on his heart. That kind of selective acceptance of prophetic messages is harmful to both the doctrine and credibility of the Christian message.

The Bible is also clear the prophetic visions had an end-point in God's plan. That end-point occurred around the time that Jesus opened the way of salvation. Zechariah said:

> On *that day* there shall be a fountain opened for the house of David and the inhabitants of Jerusalem, to cleanse them from sin and uncleanness." *And on that day,* declares the LORD of hosts, I will cut off the names of the idols from the land, so that they shall be remembered no more. And *also I will remove from the land the prophets* and the spirit of uncleanness. (13:1-2)

This is not a book on the work of prophecy, but it is so very relevant for this part of the discussion. God promised that a time would come when inspired people known as "prophets" would no longer populate the world. He said it would occur "on that day" when the fountain was opened in which sins were cleansed. Jesus did that work. That fountain's waters started flowing in Acts 2. Once the message of His gospel was delivered in its fullness, God ended the work of prophets.

The same way I know that Joseph Smith was no true prophet is the same way I know that no man can tell me what God wants me to do today apart from the contents of the Bible.

To believe in these modern "prophets" opens you up to the whims of man. Jim Jones and David Koresh had power over people because they convinced others that they spoke for God. Far too many preachers manipulate the lives of their churches' members by claiming the same power to speak directly on God's behalf. The cynic in me cannot help but notice how often the "special messages" of these preachers call for the members of their churches to part with their money for the preacher's next ministry.

Even if you disagree with my statements above, take great care in listening to anyone claiming to speak as if they spoke from God. Please heed the warning of Paul about those that claim the privilege of prophetic powers:

> But even if we or an angel from Heaven should preach to you a gospel contrary to the one we preached to you, let him be

accursed. As we have said before, so now I say again: If anyone is preaching to you a gospel contrary to the one you received, let him be accursed. (Galatians 1:8-9)

Test every message you hear about your life against the Scriptures. If the message you hear about your life goes beyond what God has revealed (2 Timothy 3:16); if it is more detailed and nuanced than the Scriptures; and especially if its end compels you to part with your liberty or money, reject it. No one should trust the self-proclaimed prophet. God's written word is enough for you to find the best. God calls you by His gospel (2 Thessalonians 2:14), not your pastor. Listen to God, not man to help you find your "Canaan."

Finding Canaan – Always Do What is Right

With that said, God is active in this world. I know that God is working to accomplish His will today. He has not abdicated His role as the God that rules in the affairs of men (Daniel 4:25). He continues to have a plan for this world. I am also convinced that I, as His son, am included in this plan. I am confident that you believe the same about yourself.

The real challenge is knowing your place in God's plan. I am confident that you want to find the best. You want to find your "Canaan." Abraham had a direct edict from God: "Leave Ur." Neither of us has that same clarity. Without that direct message from God, how can we know where "Canaan" is?

I cannot tell you directly where your "Promised Land" is. God could. However, He is not going to appear along the path of your life with a host of brightly shining angels to point it out either. Yet, you can still find it.

Just as I am convinced that God is active in the world, I am also certain of another point: The providence and guidance of God works. If God wants or needs us in a certain place, He will find the way to make that happen. The beginning point of this journey to your "Canaan" is in trusting that thought.

God has already mapped out the course to where He wants you to go. At a basic level, your only job is not to frustrate that plan by disobeying Him. The first leg on Abraham's journey was simply to leave Ur. God did not immediately tell him where to go. He just said, "Leave." The only wrong step that Abraham could have taken was to stay in Ur. His job was to keep walking and put Ur behind him until God said more about his destination. As long as Abraham keeps walking, the responsibility to direct his steps is in God's hands.

Your challenge is no different. For most of the decisions you face in your life, there is no immediate moral crisis in them. God has not told you to be a doctor and not a lawyer. He did not tell you to live in the United States and not the United Kingdom. We will address those kinds of decisions shortly. For now, let us lay those aside. God has not spoken about them to us.

Nevertheless, there are others. There are instances when we are confronted with right and wrong choices. We face moral and ethical dilemmas. What do we do then? That is an easy answer. We just do what is right. Do what is right every time.

Make this your commitment. Every time that you are confronted with a choice to accept a moral challenge to your faith or to turn away from it, accept the challenge. Always choose to do the right thing.

Beyond that, trust that God is leading you toward the best. You cannot see tomorrow. You cannot know even the consequences of your actions today. However, you can see the test to your faith that is right in front of you. God has already told you what He wants for that. The response you need is in His word. If you have a relationship in trouble, your response is not far from the Golden Rule. If you see a person in need, His call is for you to give as He gave. If you see a sinner drowning in his sin, your response is to speak a word in God's name.

The path to "Canaan" is made up of thousands of those small steps taken under the guidance of God's word. Each time your faith finds fulfillment in accepting the challenge you move closer to that spiritual home and friendship with God.

I have no great answer about the plan of God for your life. I do not even have it for my own. I do know it is always right to do right, that God rules in this world and that He is calling me to my "Canaan." All of that leads me to this confidence for me and for you, if we will always choose the right, God will direct our lives so that our steps find their rest with Him in the "Promised Land."

Finding Canaan – Do What is Meaningful

Your journey to your "Canaan" begins with choosing the right. The path does not end there. A slave can follow orders and do everything right, but still not be the friend of which we speak.

In friendship, there is trust. As we move forward in Abraham's life, we will begin to see that trust manifest itself in his life. God begins to inform Abraham of His plans because of the depth of that trust (Genesis 18:17-18). Trust implies liberty. The person given the trust is given autonomy as far as the trust goes. As a child matures in the home, he is given more freedom of action. He is allowed to be away from the home and his parents more frequently and for longer periods of time. The degree to which his parents trust him is the degree to which they provide him the freedom to go and live as he pleases.

I believe this concept is critical in understanding friendship with God. There is a reason God has not specified every action of your life. The reason is God trusts you. He has equipped us with the principles of godly living and told us to go live in this world and we have. We have spread across the globe and taken up every different occupation imaginable to man. Among the lowliest of day-workers and leaders of state, God's people are found. Each in his own circumstances can live according to the gospel and find friendship with God. This is our trust.

The concept of personal liberty that grows from an appreciation of God's trust in us is important in discussing our ability to find Canaan. Doing what is right always leads to a good life, but that may not be the best. Finding the best means engaging your spirit in striving for more. The task is active and arduous. The call is to personal responsibility, not passivity. Sitting back and waiting for the best to come will never lead you to it. If you want to find your "Canaan," you had better start looking for it with all of your energy.

Finding Canaan – A Case Study

Imagine for a moment that you are a doctor. You have spent years of your life training for the great challenge of that discipline. Why did you choose such a hard life? I am sure some do it for money or prestige. You chose that hard path because of your faith. Helping others in need awakened the urgency of responsibility within your heart. You chose it in view of your relationship to God.

With that thought, imagine further that you are happily working in an established practice. Life is good. You make a nice living, provide for your family and give generously to the Lord's work as He has blessed you. You lead your family to be spiritual people. Your life is an example of everything a Christian should be as a doctor. You never need to change one thing to live the rest of your life in a way pleasing to God. Everything is good.

Then, one Sunday at worship a missionary visits to discuss the needs of some undeveloped country across the ocean. Inside of you, your conscience sparks with a new, small flicker, "I could help them." In that moment, you realize there is another path you could take. Later that night, your mind churns over all of the pros and cons of the thought too frightening to voice.

Hearing the call of your conscience means turning your life upside down by walking away from everything you have built. Without realizing it you have entered into a crisis of faith.

You have heard missionaries in the past and done nothing. Your faith was not ready. God can use only those people who are ready to do His work and so God's call could not reach you. This time it did. You are different now. This time you realized that your best was only the good. You now see a new best on the horizon.

Will you heed its call? The choice is entirely in your hands. God never commanded you to go. You will not have violated His law in any way by staying home. What you see is just an opportunity. When you awaken on Monday, you can go to the office, go back to work, and do good for all of your patients. In time, last night's voice will wane, but your spiritual growth will never be the same. You will still be God's faithful child, but it will take longer now to be His friend. Your hesitation has done nothing to endanger your soul. But the delay has hindered your growth spiritually. You may never be the person you could have been.

What held you back from acting does not matter. You may have chosen to stay with life as it is because your obligations to family, your commitments to your practice or even your church. All of these ties are good and wholesome. Nevertheless, the dream for the best will not wait. Your mind has now seen you live a different spiritual life. No matter how good your life has been, it may never be as meaningful again. Once the spirit sees the best, the good is no longer good enough.

Or, you can go. You can go because God would go, and you have grown to be like Him. In that growth, you have seen the needs of impoverished people as He would see them. You can no more sit at home than Jesus could have stayed in Heaven. This change in you means facing new challenges. There are new fearful obstacles to be met and overcome. None of that matters. You are going to go. Your friendship with God allows for nothing else.

Finding Canaan – A Plea to Go

That is how Canaan is found. We have to do what is meaningful. Once our faith grows to the point that it sees new needs in others or new possibilities of service for ourselves, we have to act. We have to accept the challenge.

As we have said, yours will not be mine, nor mine yours. You may be called to missions, I may be called to teach and yet another will find meaning in benevolence. One doctor is called to a foreign land, and another is called by his conscience to stay at home. They are all good works. God needs all of them to be done. His body grows as each one of us supplies what our conscience is pulling us to do. He needs all of us. All of us must be true to the longing that burns inside us.

Each of us has some sense of "ought" within. There is something that we know we could and should do. We may not have ever intended to see it. The pull we are feeling may not be our "passion" in life. But it will not go away. In our dreams, both day and night, there it is. Faith has moved us to realize a great need around us. Its call will not let us go. Faith is urging us, sometimes against our preferences, toward the best. In moments of honest reflection, we know that call is one we must heed.

What is it? Right now, there is something in your life you are needing to do. Just last week or yesterday or last night in your prayers to God, there was some dream in your heart. Some dream that you are afraid to utter even to your closest friend. Your faith has been calling you to act on a vision of service.

Do not allow fear or doubt to turn you away from it. The desire in your heart comes from the agreement with God we have been discussing. Your vision makes the world as you know it appear less than it was meant to be. That it is your vision means that you can see yourself doing that very thing. It means that your faith is ready to seek

61

for a new best in your life. You know that there is more to be gained in this life. You have agreement with God about this world, yourself, and His plans for the best.

The call your heart is making is the call to "Canaan." The beckoning is not being heard by a servant, steward, or even a son. There is no command ordering you to heed this call. You violate His law in no way by ignoring what your soul is hearing. This call comes from within you because of the impact of faith in your life. Your heart is simply longing to live like God. You are being drawn by the call of friendship. Listen to it. Your spirit knows where the best is. Today is the day to take one more step to your "Canaan." You cannot stay in "Ur" any longer. Leave the good behind and go seize the best.

4

GIVING AWAY CANAAN
FOLLOWING GOD'S EXAMPLE
(GENESIS 13:1-18)

We cannot stand where God stands until we give like God gives.

I met Kevin when I was 14. His family moved from Las Vegas to West Palm Beach and started attending the church that Julie and I did. He fell into a gap that sometimes occurs in church youth groups. He was two years older than we were and there were not many teens of his age. So, he ended up being drawn into our group. With Kevin added to Jimmy, our quartet was set for the remaining days of our high school life.

Adding a 16 year old to our group was critically important. He could drive. Quickly, he was our de facto leader. I assure you that the fact that his first car was a 1967 Ford Mustang with the high-performance 289 engine had no influence on my becoming his friend. Ford had made a gorgeous and fast car, though.

No, what made Kevin such a dear friend was his heart. He had the loud, fast car. His hair was too long for some. His taste in music veered toward heavy metal choices that some deemed out of place in a church group. But his heart was among the most genuine and giving I have ever known.

His goodness was actually part of the problem. Giving to him was amazingly difficult. He drove Julie and Jimmy and me to and from every outing. He would try to pay at every meal. Coming from him, generosity was not manipulative, controlling, or needy. It was just who he was. When he had friends, he wanted to make sure he showed them how much they meant to him.

Over time that can have an impact on the recipient of the gifts. When you are always the recipient of gifts, you begin to feel small or guilty. You become sensitive to the thought that you are taking advantage of another's generosity. I know that was never his intent, but it can be tough to maintain a relationship with someone who will never let you share in the sacrifice of friendship.

We did eventually solve the problem. Kevin's job was delivering pizzas. Quite often, his nightly tips would be scattered on the seats and floorboards of his car. Since he would never take any money from us, we just started dropping cash in his car from time to time. I'm still not sure if he ever caught on to us. All I know is that it felt good to be able to give back a gift to a dear friend.

Abraham Gave Away Canaan

The spirit that was in Kevin's heart is one of the hardest lessons to teach a child. As a young boy, I used to hate that chewing gum came in packs of five pieces. With three siblings, when I opened a new pack of gum, four pieces were gone immediately. Since I was the youngest, I had little assurance of receiving the fifth piece. The lesson only grows more challenging to accept as the value of the possession in question goes up.

The high value of what is given is what makes Genesis 13 remarkable in the life of Abraham. He had been called out of Ur as we discussed in the last chapter. The call to Canaan had only been realized in Genesis 12. He had just gotten there when trouble arose.

Abraham's nephew, Lot, had accompanied him to Canaan and that act created strife in their lives. Both men were growing in wealth. They grew to the point that the portion of Canaan in which they had chosen to settle could no longer support both of their flocks. This contest for resources led to conflict among their families.

Abraham knew this condition was harmful to his family and offered Lot a gracious solution. Genesis 13:8-9 reads:

Then Abram said to Lot, "Let there be no strife between you and me, and between your herdsmen and my herdsmen, for we are kinsmen. Is not the whole land before you? Separate yourself from me. If you take the left hand, then I will go to the right, or if you take the right hand, then I will go to the left."

His solution was to give. He would give Lot whatever portion of the land he chose. Naturally, Lot chose the greenest pastures and moved toward the lush Jordan Valley and the cities of Sodom and Gomorrah. While that move did not work out well for Lot, the lesson of Abraham's example is powerful. Consider what that meant to Abraham's life. God had called him away from his family and his home. He was called with the promise of being shown a great land that would be his. Before he pitched his tent fully, he was challenged to give it away.

Friendship Needs Mutual Sacrifice

Friendship needs giving. An important tie exists between these two concepts. On a basic level, giving is the definition of friendship. Our friends give to us, and we give to our friends. Separating the two in your thinking is impossible. How could someone possibly be your friend if you were unwilling to give anything to him?

Friendship needs giving because giving is an investment in another person. When you sacrifice out of your goods and energies for another's benefit, you are investing in his well-being. You are making a statement that you value that individual enough to sacrifice for his benefit. Your actions are a testimony to the depth of his need and the worth of his person.

Investment creates attachment. When you purchase a few shares of a company's stock, you suddenly follow that business' progress more intensely. You cannot just turn away because you now have something of value at risk. The same is true with people. Giving to another person personally invests your life in his. Your stake creates the same kind of attachment. The more you work with and give to him, the closer you are drawn to him.

Nevertheless, we need to understand that action is only a one-way action. Giving to another draws you to another person, but receiving a gift does not always move the recipient closer to the giver. The recipient of a gift has nothing invested in the life of the giver. His tie is only to the gift given. Do you think that is harsh? Well, it is. But it is true. Solomon said, "Wealth brings many new friends, but a poor man is deserted by his friend" (Proverbs 19:4).

Our celebrity-crazed society highlights the fickleness of relationships built on one-way giving. Just in recent years the fall of Mel Gibson, Michael Vick, and Tiger Woods shows how quickly people will desert a benefactor as soon as their wealth or reputation is lost. I am confident that in each of those cases, those icons of popularity believed they had more friends than they truly did. Each was wealthy and esteemed beyond the dreams of normal people. That wealth of material and ethereal riches accumulated legions of followers. Their entourages responded to their every desire, while the celebrities' positions provided their "friends" with an incredible lifestyle.

What about now? Where are they now that each has the façade of his image broken? Mr. Gibson will never be the star he once was. Mr. Vick is playing again, but the "Michael Vick Experience" is forever gone. Tiger was not only the best golfer in the world but also the icon of discipline and focus. He may return to winning tournaments again, but the truth of his normalcy and humanity has been exposed. Now that they are no longer perfect, will their "friends" ever return? No, they will not. Their entourages were never invested in the celebrity. The gifts were never repaid. They were never true friends. One-way relationships never create friendships.

This principle is just as true for us. Have you ever had someone in your life that needed constant attention? In time, that kind of person begins to annoy. He was taking more than he was giving. Your investment in him was much larger than his investment in you. You may even have cared more about the outcome your gift created than did the person to whom you gave it.

Friendship needs mutual investment. Friendship exists between equal partners who share and give freely. It thrives on communion. That common act creates a mutual tie. Each time a gift is given the bond grows stronger. Only in a relationship of open and mutual giving can true friendship be forged.

Giving With God

The word "God" and forms of "give" are directly connected about 400 times in the English Bible. Everything from our world, to our souls, to His only Son is given to us by God. Paul well described our relationship to Him in Acts 17:28: "In him we live and move and have our being."

It is difficult to conceive of a child of God who does not understand this thought. Every good thing we are or have comes from God's sacrificing for us. He is invested in us. Psalm 8 declares that He is "mindful" of man. Ephesians 1:18 says that God possesses an inheritance in (notice "in" to "for") His saints: "Having the eyes of your hearts enlightened, that you may know what is the hope to which he has called you, what are the riches of his glorious inheritance in the saints."

A common adage states that you tell how much something is worth by seeing what someone is willing to pay for it. When you apply that consideration to God's work with humanity, His level of attachment to mankind is staggering. He created the universe in all its glory in order to give it to man. He furnished our world with its overflowing bounty so that man could partake of His goodness. Then, God emptied Heaven of its greatest treasure to redeem man back to Himself.

In our relationship to God, He is always the giver.

Giving Back to God

If our premise that friendship needs mutual sacrifice is true, then we have a problem. How can man possibly give anything of value to God? There is no way to enter into anything approaching a partnership of giving with Him. His ability to give will infinitely surpass ours. His lack of any need will never provide us any opportunity to give anyway. There is nothing mutual about it.

We do give to God, true. In every section of Scripture, man is busily making offerings to Him. Nevertheless, there is a difference between making an obligatory offering to the Master and sacrificing of our own treasures to meet the need of a friend. We do the former every day as we live in His service. We can never do the latter. God has no needs that we can meet.

There is our problem. We are always in a position of being the recipients of God's blessings. He gives to us, and we get from Him. In every friendship there must be that mutual give and take. Between friends, the gifts given may not be the same, but there are always times when one needs the other. A wealthy friend may give money to his poorer friend's financial need, and the poor friend may return that gift with counsel, companionship, and loyalty. Both are giving and so are invested in the relationship. If only one gives, there is no friendship, only a relationship of convenience and gain.

Perhaps some have a relationship with God based on gain. They will serve Him so long as they perceive His blessings in their lives. Then, if the time comes when following Him no longer is profitable, they will turn to other sources for their gifts. There is no friendship there. They are exactly like the gold-diggers who latch on to athletes, celebrities, and the wealthy. Their interest is purely in gain.

How is it possible to have anything approaching friendship with God if He needs nothing from us?

Why We Give – To be Transformed

I believe the answer is not to give *to* God but to give *with* God. There is an interesting dynamic in the New Testament about giving. Scripture tells us to give continually. However, have you ever noticed that we are rarely instructed about how to give?

Look at three verses with me and notice that in each of these verses, there is an imperative statement about our sharing of our blessings with others, but there is no statement as to how much and how often it is to be done.

Look first at Ephesians 4:28: "Let the thief no longer steal, but rather let him labor, doing honest work with his own hands, so that he may have something to share with anyone in need."

The purpose of work is to have something to share: How much? How often? To what degree? To what extent? It is unqualified.

Next look at James 2:15-16, that great passage examining the relationship of faith and works:

> If a brother or sister is poorly clothed and lacking in daily food, and one of you says to them, "Go in peace, be warmed and filled," without giving them the things needed for the body, what good is that?

Again, notice there is in that verse the concept of the obligation that a child of God has to meet the needs of those that are around them. Again, to what degree, to what extent or how often? No quantification is stated expressly.

Also 1 John 3:16-18 has the same kind of statement:

> By this we know love, that he laid down his life for us, and we ought to lay down our lives for the brothers. But if anyone has the world's goods and sees his brother in need, yet closes his heart against him, how does God's love abide in him? Little children, let us not love in word or talk but in deed and in truth.

Again, "give" when you see someone in need. How much, to what extent, how often?

Repeatedly, the Christian is expected to be a giver. Our responsibility goes far beyond the commands to give an offering to God. We do ourselves harm when we boil down the Christian's responsibility to give as a part of worship each week. That is only a small portion of our giving. Christians are to have a life of giving. We are to be people who have a nature of giving. If we only think about it in terms of our weekly offering, we have missed a great lesson.

Giving's focus also encompasses our relationship with God. Sharing the blessings of God with others is not just about the people with whom we share them. Yes, every time we give of ourselves or share our resources with another, they benefit from the offering. They will see your good works, and they in turn will be thankful back to God. Giving helps the recipient, but that is not its primary benefit. There is a greater blessing in giving than receiving (Acts 20:35). Giving helps the recipient, but it transforms the giver. God always gives. To have that same nature which seeks to supply the needs of others is the transformation we are seeking in order to become God's friend.

We are trying to grow spiritually to become friends with God. In order for a servant to become a son, to become a friend, God must transform the servant who is focused on pleasing the master in obedience into a friend whose focus has been elevated to see opportunities just as He sees them. If God is always a giver, in order to be His friends we need to be people who give naturally – not out of duty, debt or obligation. We need to give because it is the natural expression of our hearts when we see someone else in need. We respond to that need just as He would respond to that need.

He needs us to give out of the same motivation as He does. Why did God send Jesus? That question has a simple answer, "For God so loved the world that he sent" – that He gave, that He shared. God did it because He loved us. He did it because He thought we were worthy. Our Lord valued us as people. He wanted to help us. No one had to tell Him it had to be done. He did not do it out of obligation. Helping those in need is a true expression of His character. God always gives.

God is trying to move us toward the ideal of giving. He does not want us to see the blessings in our lives as an end. We need to see them as a means. God gives to us for the sole reason so we can give to others. When we respond in harmony with that intention, not out of duty or obligation, but out of instinct then our souls have become like His and we stand alongside Him in a fellowship of giving.

To Stand With God, Be a Giver

"*We cannot stand where God stands until we give as God gives,*" is the lesson of Genesis 13. Abraham's offering to Lot is an example of how one man joined with God in giving. God gave Canaan to Abraham. However, the gift was never for Abraham. His descendants would not claim the land until centuries after the patriarch's death. Even after they did, that blessing was still not for them. The promise to Abraham in Genesis 12 did not point to Abraham. God's words did not point just to a blessing for Abraham or just for his family. The blessing was for all nations. Abraham was placed in Canaan ultimately so that Jesus would have a home. Abraham could never have seen the fullness of the blessings that God had planned for him. Nevertheless, his attitude toward those blessings was exactly the attitude that God needed him to have so that He could bring that fullness into Abraham's life.

Abraham viewed the land of Canaan not as a reward, but as a tool that he could use to bless his nephew. The land was the means that he chose to use to achieve a godly end – peace within his family. Abraham did with the Promised Land just what God had done with that treasure. He used that promised land to benefit someone else. More importantly, in using it to benefit someone else, he used it to highlight for his nephew that the spiritual blessings of family are of more value than the best that the world has to offer. Unfortunately, Lot seems to have missed the lesson.

That Lot missed the lesson is not important. What is important to see is that the motivation behind the gift of Canaan was the same for God and Abraham. God sacrificed the Promised Land by devoting it to the use of one family. So too, Abraham sacrificed his possession of the Promised Land for the benefit of a part of his family. Surely, the scale is different. God's action is one that is eternal and infinite in its significance. God's gift would result in all of humanity being blessed. Abraham's gift is local and transient in the life of Lot. Yet, the motivation of character is the same. By seeing others in the same light as God saw them, Abraham shared in a fellowship of giving with God.

We would do well to learn that same lesson in giving. Selfishness, covetousness, and materialism are all dead-ends. They all seek to accumulate possessions. Once the possessions are acquired, what next? If our mindset is that of a collector of this world's goods, we have become just like an entourage surrounding a celebrity. We sit back and wait for our Benefactor to bless us. We wait for Him to add another item to our collection – another gift to add to our stores. With that mindset, we can never become like God.

We cannot stand where God stands. We will freely admit that He blesses us. God gives us opportunity. He gives us the wealth that we have. In so doing, we admit that we have not become like Him. He gave, but too often, we hoard. God saw His blessings as tools to enrich and uplift others – us. We saw in those blessings security, prosperity, and comfort for ourselves. Friendship demands mutual sacrifice. Every time He blesses us, He has chosen to use what He has created for us and for our well-being. In order to become His friend, we must see those same opportunities in those blessings. The fact that the scale of our ability to give can never equal God's scale does not matter. Our friendship with God is not based on the grandeur of the scale of our gifts. It is based on communion of character. To be His friends, we must commune in the fellowship of those blessings.

Nevertheless, we must ask again: "How much, to what extent, and how often?" At some point we ask that. I believe that we all believe that it is more "blessed to give than it is to receive." Our challenge is that giving is always frightening. There has to be limits, right? If we give away all that we have, what will we have left to care for our own needs?

To be fair, there are other obligations that God has given us to meet with the blessings He gives us. Just look in 1 Timothy 5:8: "But if anyone does not provide for his relatives, and especially for members of his household, he has denied the faith and is worse than an unbeliever."

That does not suggest that Christians ought to give away all their possessions to the point that they become paupers or to sacrifice all their time and energies until they lose their individuality and identity. There must be a balance in all things. Yet, there is a truth about giving that we must accept if we are ever to become God's friend. The axiom is highlighted so poignantly in Abraham's life – God always honors and repays gifts offered in His name.

God Always Protects the Giver

Abraham does not appear to be the kind of man that would wallow in self-pity or regret over his decision. Abraham's offering is nothing but the genuine expression of concern for his nephew. Nevertheless, Canaan is now gone. If Lot is successful in the best part of the land, Lot's herds are going to grow. He is going to become more wealthy. Lot's descendants would build cities and populate the Promised Land. There is a real danger in the sacrifice Abraham is making. Even as grand as the land was, it had fixed borders. There were a finite number of acres in it. Every acre taken and used by Lot's descendants was one less available to Abraham and his seed. There was a real danger that Lot's family and not Abraham's would establish their claim to the Promised Land.

Just as a parent praises the offering of his generous child as soon as the gift is given, God moved quickly to show Abraham that would not

72

happen. Abraham had given his inheritance away. No sooner had Lot moved his herds to the choicest part of Canaan, than God appeared to Abraham. Lot took the best, but God appears to Abraham. God had to show him that nothing he had given away was lost:

> The LORD said to Abram, after Lot had separated from him, "Lift up your eyes and look from the place where you are, northward and southward and eastward and westward, for all the land that you see I will give to you and to your offspring forever. I will make your offspring as the dust of the earth, so that if one can count the dust of the earth, your offspring also can be counted. Arise, walk through the length and the breadth of the land, for I will give it to you." So Abram moved his tent and came and settled by the oaks of Mamre, which are at Hebron, and there he built an altar to the LORD. (Genesis 13:14-18)

Nothing had changed. Abraham had lost nothing by giving.

God's blessings are not finite. They are infinite. God's answer to Abraham's choice was not to take away the Promised Land from His friend. His response was to increase the outpouring of His blessings. Once Abraham gifted a part of the land to his nephew, God honored that choice. Not only that, God remember it 400 years later when He brought Abraham's descendants into the land. There is an amazing statement by Moses in the book of Deuteronomy as He is giving the Israelites the final instruction about how they are to conduct themselves in the land:

> And the LORD said to me, "Do not harass Moab or contend with them in battle, for I will not give you any of their land for a possession, because I have given Ar to *the people of Lot* for a possession." (Deuteronomy 2:9)

Moab was one of Lot's sons. Because Abraham had blessed Lot by giving him the land, God protected and honored that gift. God's answer to Abraham's gift was, "Abraham, if you are going to take the blessings that I have given you and share them with someone else, I am just going to increase the blessing. Not only will you have the Promised Land, but I will give Lot the land of Moab."

God's response is to give the land of Moab to Lot. He made provisions for both of them. God gave to Abraham, and Abraham gave to Lot. Instead of taking away from Abraham, God simply increased His blessings. God's blessings do not come from a bucket with a bottom in them. The fountain of God's blessings would supply all that Abraham would ever need. They are infinite, "The steadfast love of the LORD never ceases; his mercies never come to an end; they are new every morning; great is your faithfulness" (Lamentations 3:22-23).

Giving never diminishes us. Every time we pass on to another the drink we each have received from the living fountain of God's blessings, God quickly refills our empty vessel. However, we are always transformed in giving. Giving always changes the giver. Every time it is done, our sharing makes us more like our God and moves us closer to friendship. The path to friendship is made up with thousands of steps taken in the guidance of faith. Countless of them begin right here with this concept. Are we willing to share and to give our time, our energy, our emotions, our money, our creativity? They all seem so important to us. As we expend them on others, it is tempting to think that there we will be nothing left for ourselves.

There is no danger in giving. God will keep us safe as we sacrifice with Him. God's fountain is still flowing. We need to keep on giving. God has blessed His people so richly. This world needs what we have. Do not worry. When you give away, God will provide more. Along the way, His blessings will transform us into His friends as those blessings pass from His hands through our hands and then on to someone else.

The Best Comes Through Giving

"We cannot stand where God stands until we give as God gives." That phrase well summarizes the lesson we have seen in Genesis 13. However, before we pass from it, we must see the connection between that thought and the overall point of this study of Abraham that "Faith fulfilled ends in friendship."

Giving is commanded of us because the action was precious to God. The life of Abraham in the Bible begins with a promise of giving from God. There is no right understanding of God that excludes His selflessness toward us. Generosity flows freely from His character of love. In that sense, His nature demanded that He create the world and then sacrifice His Son to protect it. God will always give.

The transformation that occurs in giving is the engine that will fulfill our faith and transform us into being God's friend. I believe that is why, once out of Ur and its entanglements, that Abraham must demonstrate His willingness to sacrifice the Promised Land. Every challenge he will face from Genesis 13 forward will be met by being willing to subjugate his own needs to another's. Exalting what others need or desire above your own is the motivation behind every act of godly giving.

In our journey to friendship with God, or as we called it in the last chapter, the journey from the good to the best, every step in the journey is an act of sacrifice. Trading in your good for a new challenge toward the best is an act that endangers your stability and comfort. The only motivation that will sustain the progress of such harrowing decisions is a developing awareness of how much the people around us need and deserve the touch of God in their lives that can only come through the hands of His people.

Stated simply, only the people who are willing to give like God gives will ever be able to stand beside Him as friends. This selfless nature will carry Abraham's faith along in the pages to come. When it is present in our faith, it will bring us closer to our best every day.

Let's be people like Abraham, who don't hoard the blessings of God but give them freely to accomplish spiritual ends. Freely we have received, freely we must give.

PART 3 - I AM GOD'S SON

Sons have freedom that servants do not. They have promises from their fathers. The fathers are even obligated to care for them. The father is responsible for his son's having life and so he is invested in helping his son be successful in life. Jesus made clear the distinction between servants and sons: "The slave does not remain in the house forever; the son remains forever" (John 8:35).

Sons are still subject to correction and punishment for missteps. However, their ordinary failures will never result in their being cast out of the father's house. Sonship is a privileged position. Sons never have to prove their worth. They do not have to earn their place in the family by serving out of duty and fear.

The step from servant to son is too important to miss. In order to make that step, we have to trust that our Father will accept us and approve of us even when we cannot see or understand what He wants.

In Part 3, Abraham teaches us this lesson. Through Genesis 15-17, Abraham moves from obedience to participation. God's direction progresses from "Go and I will," in Genesis 12-13 to "This is my covenant, which you shall keep, between me and you and your offspring" (17:10). Abraham goes from following behind God to being responsible for maintaining the purity of their relationship through circumcision. He has become a son, trusted to participate in the actions of His Father. His example calls us to follow.

5

WAITING FOR ISAAC
FREE TO QUESTION
(GENESIS 15:1-11)

Faith does not exclude doubt

My path to preaching began with an old 8088 IBM PC and a Hayes Smartmodem. I hate how old this next sentence is going to make me sound, but . . . back in the days before the internet, private individuals hosted their own "sites" using something known as the BBS (bulletin board system). Those BBS's were not typically linked to any other site. Each BBS had its own phone number that you called to log in to the board. Given that most commonly these sites were run out of people's homes and over their home phone lines, only one person could be on the site at a time. The browsing was amazingly slow. At best, my modem could maintain a connection that could transmit about 300 characters per second and that speed was more theoretical than real. To put that in perspective, that is about three lines of typed text per second. You needed to be a true geek to be interested and dedicated enough to persevere. These sites functioned much like the messages boards and forums that are a part of most major websites today. While there were no graphics (unless you consider carefully arranged ASCII characters as art) and few of the convenient features of today's site were available, the BBS's worked well enough to communicate with others.

In the church I attended there was a man we all called "Buzz." He hosted his own bulletin board out of his home. The site was his ministry and is largely responsible for mine now. His site was an active one for the time and was filled with religious discussions. The activity and topics were engaging. I began to take part in those discussions of apologetics and salvation. I quickly realized how powerful being engaged in spiritual endeavors can be in your life.

That focus on spiritual things began to spill over from the fledgling "cyber" world into my daily walk. My dialogue with my co-workers became more spiritually focused. I found a segment of co-workers that welcomed the encouragement and challenge that comes with the meeting of divergent beliefs about the Bible.

As the weeks and months passed my spirit's message slowly penetrated my consciousness. I did not know it then, but I can see it now, I was looking for the best. I had found a new way of living and growing in faith that needed to be explored. Giving my life to the preaching of the gospel was the only answer to the longing.

That time was more than twenty years ago and that same desire is alive within me. There is nothing that I enjoy more than teaching the Bible. As the members of the church where I teach can attest, I can go on and on in discussing questions about God and His word. When someone is wanting to learn more about some spiritual truth there is almost no limit to the enthusiasm that I have to engage with him in that discussion.

That is true for every person in my life but one. Julie can frustrate me with a Bible question faster than any person I know. She has an uncanny knack for phrasing her thoughts or persisting in an inquiry in just the perfect way to stir my emotions. She knows there is no distance between us. There is no reason for her not to press on in trying to understand something I am saying. When others, just out of the pressure of social norms, might end their questions, Julie knows no reason for any reservation. She is assured that her persistence or the liberty she takes in her questions will have no repercussions on the state of our love for each other. That knowledge provides her confidence to say whatever is on her heart. If she does not understand or agree with an answer I have given, she has complete freedom to voice that feeling. Unrestrained liberty of expression is one of the privileges of intimate friendship. Apparently, I still have a lot of work to do on myself because Julie's use of that freedom can still make me crazy.

God Allows Questions

Immersing yourself in the story is a critical tool in Bible study. Imagining yourself in the place of the characters and feeling what they felt and seeing what they saw brings Bible stories to life. I think that is why Mel Gibson's *Passion of the Christ* from several years ago struck such a chord with people. His vision of those events may not have been perfect (No person's vision could have been perfect.), but it was clear enough that it allowed many people to place themselves in a Bible story in ways they had never done so before. For most viewers, the experience was powerful.

One of the great challenges in doing that for yourself is grasping the passing of time in the lives of Bible characters. In coming to an understanding of Abraham's life, it is important that we meet this difficulty. From his introduction in Genesis 12 to the birth of Isaac, Abraham's life spans about 25 years. Including the time up to the sacrifice of his son in chapter 22 increases that number upwards of 40 years. Yet the Bible covers those four decades in fewer than 7,000 words.

Consider how little we actually know about this man's life. Those 7,000 words give us insight into just a handful of days of his life. I have tried to count how many times we are told what he did on a specific day. I cannot get the count over about two dozen. Of the 36,500 days (or so) leading Abraham up to the birth of his promised son, God reveals only twenty or so special days for us.

As we read his life, we pass over wide gaps of time in just sentences – gaps of time that when they happen in our lives are meaningful. The passage of a decade changes us. We age. We mature. Our faith is different. Often, we struggle. Sometimes the slow progress of time creates doubt about ourselves and God when problems that we thought would be over quickly linger and linger.

Abraham's Question

Abraham was no different. Time impacted him and his faith just as it does ours. As he left Ur, his eyes were looking for the city of God (Hebrews 11:10). The hope of great things buoyed his faith even as he left his home and family behind. He has suffered through famine, gone through his conflict with Lot and given away the better portion of the land. He has fought in his first war and come away victorious. At the close of chapter 14, Abraham is still wholly reliant on God and trusting fully in God's promises and ability to provide for him. His words to the king of Sodom at the end of that chapter show a man strong in his conviction of trust in God:

> But Abram said to the king of Sodom, "I have lifted my hand to the LORD, God Most High, Possessor of Heaven and earth, that I would not take a thread or a sandal strap or anything that is yours, lest you should say, 'I have made Abram rich.'" (Genesis 14:22-23)

His God is the possessor of Heaven and earth. Nothing is beyond His power. Yet in the midst of all of this, he has been told that the land is going to be his and given to his descendants after him, and therein is the seed of the problem. Abraham has no son, and he is already an old man. Time is about to turn that seed into a tree, laden with fruit.

In Genesis 15, Abraham's faith begins to feast on the fruit of that doubt. He openly calls God's plan into question. The change between his unassailable confidence in chapter 14 ("God Most High, Possessor of Heaven and Earth" – the One that will make Abraham rich) and his open doubt in the very next verses is abrupt and seems disjointed at first reading.

Until we realize that the events of chapter 15 occur up to a decade after the close of chapter 14. Genesis 16:3 makes mention of that length of time passing since Abraham and Sarah had entered Canaan: "After Abram had lived ten years in the land of Canaan, Sarai, Abram's wife, took Hagar the Egyptian, her servant, and gave her to Abram her husband as a wife."

Abraham's doubt in chapter 15 leads him to offer Eliezer as his son. Sarah's plan in chapter 16 is to present Hagar to Abraham to produce a son. The struggle of faith is the same in each of these instances. That makes it likely that the events of chapter 15 occur much closer to chapter 16 than chapter 13. Working with that thought, upwards of ten years in Abraham's journey with God have passed between God's first appearance to Abraham in the Promised Land (chapter 13) and His second appearance (chapter 15).

Ten years have gone by. What has changed? His entrance into the land had been a tsunami of activity. Famine, political intrigue, family conflict, war, and victory had all been his. But then what? Lot's moving away had cut the final cord with his family. The battle he had fought for Lot had created new enemies in the land. A decade has passed. He is alone. He owns no land. Worse still, there is no child – no seed. Abraham is now in his middle-80's. He has reason to be concerned. His doubts and questions are legitimate.

Given the opportunity, Abraham openly expresses those reservations. I am confident that it came as no surprise to God – nothing does. In fact, looking at the words God uses to begin this next encounter with Abraham, it is clear He was anticipating Abraham's reservations: "After these things the word of the LORD came to Abram in a vision: "*Fear not, Abram, I am your shield; your reward shall be very great.*" (Genesis 15:1)

His opening remarks to Abraham are remarks of promised protection and a reassurance that the promise has not been forgotten. In chapter 14, Abraham's concern was that it might appear that another man and not God had made him rich (14:23). Abraham was gaining much in the way of wealth as evidenced by the growth of his house (14:14). Yet here, that is not at all his concern. His response to God's statement that his reward "shall be very great," is focused and laced with a hint of accusation.

But Abram said, "O Lord GOD, what will *you give me*, for I continue childless, and the heir of my house is Eliezer of Damascus?" And Abram said, "Behold, *you have given me no offspring*, and a member of my household will be my heir." (Genesis 15:1-2)

"You have given me no offspring," is Abraham's sole concern. From the promise that God had made to Abraham, the missing son is the one glaring omission. At nearly 85 years of age, his mortality and the future is weighing heavily on his mind. He knows he has no child. Someone will take what he has. He wants this problem solved. Strong emotions are taking Abraham through the same worries that lay on the heart of every man and woman as they grow nearer to death. His life has been given to following this path onto which God had led him and after ten years, nothing has been solved. Can you hear the pain and worry in his voice as he asks, "What will you give me, for I continue childless?" This was God's promise and His problem to solve. Only He was not doing it.

Abraham is looking for an answer. The only solution he sees is in his steward, Eliezer. God answers the charge, "And behold, the word of the LORD came to him: 'This man shall not be your heir; your very own son shall be your heir'" (Genesis 15:4).

God's Answer to Abraham

God has a plan for Abraham, but Abraham cannot see it. The limitation of his perception leads him to question the plan. He even concocts an alternative plan for God: "I don't have a child, let's just give it to Eliezer." God replies, "No, Abraham. That is not my plan. My plan is that your own son shall be your heir." So as a part of that re-affirmation of that plan, in verse 5, God says, "And he brought him outside and said, 'Look toward Heaven, and number the stars, if you are able to number them.' Then he said to him, 'So shall your offspring be.'"

Once again, God clarifies the statement. The promise is the same one, expressed in the same words, that He made to Abraham years ago (13:16). Nothing has changed. Time has not impacted God's plan.

We might be tempted to think that Abraham would accept the plan at this point. We might think that if Abraham continued to question God, or to doubt the plan of God, that somehow Abraham would fall out of good standing with God. Would you think it right or would you dare to continue to question God after such a clear statement?

God's discussion with Abraham was no momentary, flippant re-statement of His promise. Look at verse 5 again: "And he brought him outside. . ." God took the time to walk Abraham out of his tent. With the coarse grains of sand scratching against his worn feet and his weary eyes staring into the countless points of light above him, God promised again the same blessing to Abraham.

In that scene, alone with God in the nature which was designed to show the majesty of God (Psalm 19:1-2), would you dare to question God again? Would you dare to say, "I don't believe it yet?" Abraham did. God saw it in him and continued to re-assure. This time in verse 7, He adds, "And he said to him, 'I am the LORD who brought you out from Ur of the Chaldeans to give you this land to possess.'"

Three times God had affirmed His promise of Abraham's reward to him. Three times – imagine that. Surely, for a man of faith three promises from God would be enough. It was not. Abraham was not done. His heart would not be quieted so easily. The doubt and worry of the weary servant of God still lingers in his next words: "But he said, 'O Lord GOD, how am I to know that I shall possess it?'" (Genesis 15:8).

"How can I know?" Abraham needed what we need from God – proof.

God Always Proves His Promises

Wait a minute. Did God not just tell him that if he could number the stars of Heaven then he could number his offspring?

God has already told Abraham, "I am your shield. Your reward should be great." After he questioned God the first time, God said, "Your offspring will be as numerous as the stars." Then he says, "I am the God that brought you here." Three different times in three different ways, God re-affirms the promise. Yet at the end of it Abraham, still says, "How am I to know this?" If you read it too quickly, you might miss what is going on here. Abraham is questioning God for the third time. That is nothing short of astonishing to me. God says, "Yes, I am with you."

Abraham says, "What? What will you give me?"

God says, "Everything I've promised. I'll give you the stars of Heaven."

And Abraham says, "I'm not sure."

God says "I've brought you this far, trust me for the rest."

Abraham's responds, "God, you need to prove this to me."

What is God's response? Abraham wanted proof. "How am I to trust you?"

What is God's response? Is it anger?

Your view of how God might respond to that probably says something about the way you view yourself before God. If you think that God would now show anger, you probably see yourself as His servant. If a servant questions his master repeatedly the master will get angry. Is that God with Abraham? Does Abraham's doubt heat the embers of God's wrath?

Look at what God says to Abraham's expression of doubt:

> He said to him, "Bring me a heifer three years old, a female goat three years old, a ram three years old, a turtledove, and a young pigeon." And he brought him all these, cut them in half, and laid each half over against the other. But he did not cut the birds in half. And when birds of prey came down on the carcasses, Abram drove them away. (Genesis 15:9-11)

We will discuss more about this in the next chapter, but for now know that the cutting in half of the animals was a sign that the ancients used of a binding covenant. Keil and Delitzsch make these comments regarding these verses:

> The proceeding corresponded rather to the custom, prevalent in many ancient nations, of slaughtering animals when concluding a covenant, and after dividing them into pieces, of laying the pieces opposite to one another, that the persons making the covenant might pass between them. Thus Ephraem Syrus (1, 161) observes, that God condescended to follow the custom of the Chaldeans, that He might in the most solemn manner confirm His oath to Abram the Chaldean. (214)

God comes to Abraham and does just what the ancients would have expected in order to bind oneself in a covenant with another. He takes upon himself the sign of that covenant.

Abraham's plea had been "I need proof. I need to know." God provided him exactly what he needed to "know." It is interesting that in verse 13, the Bible says, "The Lord said to Abram, 'Know for certain that your offspring will be sojourners in a land.'" And then down in verse 18, "On that day, the Lord made a covenant with Abram, saying, 'to your offspring I give this land.'" Twice more God comes back to Abraham and says, "Know this, know this."

Abraham asked the question, "How can I know?"

God's response was to give Abraham exactly what he needed: "You need to know this, Abraham, you need to know this."

What is God's response to the doubt and questioning of Abraham? His answer is to provide Abraham exactly what he needs. His friend, Abraham, is expressing doubt, frustration, and concern. What is God's reply? Neither His words, nor His actions show any hint of anger.

Anger grows out of insecurity. Have you ever had a boss that was trying to push a plan through about which you had questions? There was something in his plan that you simply did not understand, but as soon as you started questioning him about it, he became irrationally angered. He was insecure. Your boss knew there was some flaw or was afraid there might have been. Insecurity stops people from confronting the evidence. When you are right, there is no reason to get mad because you have the evidence to prove it. Anger grows out of insecurity.

Is God insecure about His plan? Does God have any doubt about what is coming for Abraham? Then why would God need to be fearful or angry about Abraham's questioning? What does God do? He quietly, in terms and actions Abraham would have understood, says, "Abraham, you need to know this. I will do anything I can to prove it to you. I will promise that I am your shield. I will remind you of the past blessings I have given to you. I will bind myself in a covenant with you. I will do whatever it takes to prove it to you."

God's response is to provide proof. His confident, calm answer shows us a great lesson about faith and our relationship with God: "*Faith does not exclude doubt.*"

Faith Does Not Exclude Doubt

This time put yourself in the place of the supervisor at work. You present a plan of action to employees that you oversee and immediately the questions start. From most of your co-workers that presents only the headache that comes from explaining yourself repeatedly. Such frustration is part of the job and it is no real problem. Then there is Tom. He thinks he knows best and will voice his opinion about that at every turn. Further, he has no respect for you or your abilities. He cannot imagine why he has to answer to you – ever. You know he is not interested in understanding your decision. He just wants to ridicule it and diminish you. Nearly every office has a 'Tom' (and far too many churches).

How do you respond to him? Given his disposition, you have to keep him on a short leash. You cannot afford to engage him in dialogue. His heart will not allow you to show him much patience. His insolence cannot be placated. Patience would only encourage him. Your response would be terse and pointed. You would appear, and indeed, may be, angry. God has responded in that way to people many times. Jesus treated the Pharisees or Sadducees or the lawyers that way often. Their questions and temptations of the Lord were often rebuked harshly. When they challenged His authority, He had no problems in dismissing them quickly: "'Tell us, then, what you think. Is it lawful to pay taxes to Caesar, or not?' But Jesus, aware of their malice, said, 'Why put me to the test, you hypocrites?'" (Matthew 22:17-18).

Abraham is not that kind of person. His question was not one of malice. When he doubted the plan of God, what was his response? Was it to give up or to turn away from God?

"God, I don't have a child."

There is the doubt. God had promised him something and he had waited a long while and did not yet have it. What did he do?

"Let me help you. Take Eliezer."

That is an amazing response: "God I can't see it. I do not know how it is going to happen. God, this cannot work. I've got another idea."

Abraham is trying to help God out. He is trying to make God's work easier. Abraham has no malice toward God. He is a friend trying to help another one out.

You have seen it in your own life. Your friend or spouse makes a promise to you and you see his struggling to carry it out. Yet because you love him, what is your response?

"Don't worry about it. It is ok. It will be all right. We can do it this way. I can help you here."

We all treat our good friends in that same manner. When you have doubts about the future, you try to work it out. You try to find another path. You try to lend any help you can.

Abraham does just that: "God, I don't see it. Let's go with Eliezer." He had no thought of impugning the character of God. Moreover, on

God's part, He could see things that Abraham could not. He was secure enough not to be threatened by that doubt. God knew Himself, His own abilities, His power, His plan, and the future. He also knew Abraham's heart:

> For I know him, that he will command his children and his household after him, and they shall keep the way of the LORD, to do justice and judgment; that the LORD may bring upon Abraham that which he hath spoken of him. (Genesis 18:19)

God knew Abraham wanted to do what was right and best. He also knew what Abraham needed. Abraham did not need anything other than knowledge. He needed to know what was going to happen, which is exactly what Genesis 15 says, "Abraham, your seed will be strangers in a foreign land. And then they will come back here and when they do they will possess it forever."

God answers the question Abraham asks. He knew that if Abraham could see what He could see, that Abraham would respond the way that God would. God gave Abraham exactly what he needed. He knew that even as Abraham's heart cried out in doubt it was still strong in faith.

You see, faith or trust in God does not mean that you cannot have doubt. The establishment of that thought is what makes Genesis 15:1-11 so powerful. We have looked at 10 of those 11 verses and each one of them is a statement of Abraham's doubts or God's handling of those doubts. It is in the one verse we skipped that the foundation of this lesson is taught.

Read Genesis 15:6: "And he believed in the LORD; and he counted it to him for righteousness." That verse is quoted in Romans 4:3. Why is that important?

It is because in Romans 4 Abraham is called the father of all who believe as he did:

> That is why it depends on faith, in order that the promise may rest on grace and be guaranteed to all his offspring--not only to the adherent of the law but also to the one who shares the faith of Abraham, who is the father of us all. (Romans 4:16)

The faith of Genesis 15 is the kind of faith that God wants us to have. I am not sure we grasp the power of that. We often take a look at Abraham's faith and see in it the great triumphs. Contemplating his life can be overwhelming. As we read about Abraham's life from Genesis 12 through Genesis 22, our minds fixate on the image of his standing on Mt. Moriah as he is offering up his son and saying, "God will provide the offering." What an amazing statement of the faith of Abraham!

That event is the one we would expect God to highlight as the power of faith. Yet, it is not the sacrifice of his son or his journey out of Ur that God uses to show the kind of faith that God wants. His moment of great faith is found right in the middle of Abraham's saying to God, "What? I have nothing. How can I know?" I do not think there is a stronger moment of doubt in the life of Abraham than Genesis 15. That moment of strongly expressed doubt is when God stops and says, "He believed me and I counted it to him for righteousness."

Faith is not the absence of doubt. Where there is no doubt there is no need for faith. Faith is the confidence to move forward in spite of doubt. Abraham could not see the fullness of God's plan nor did he know the timing. There were still many years to go before Isaac would come. In spite of those doubts, he stayed true to his commitment to his friend.

True Friendship Means Freedom of Expression

Do not read through this text and miss the application of this lesson to the development of your faith. True friendship means there is freedom of expression.

Communication is the greatest need in any continuing relationship. Any time I have had the opportunity to be involved in relationship counseling, the root of the problem usually worked back to communication. Unless there is some deep-seated sinfulness in one's heart, the problems in marriage began because there was an absence of good communication. They were not hearing each other. Over time, those layers of insensitivity began to build up and up and now the couple is so far apart it is almost impossible to put them back together. The core of it was that either one party or the other (or both) was not free to say, "This is how I'm feeling" and have the other person hear him and respond to it.

If you do not have a freedom of expression, a freedom of communication in your relationship, the relationship is doomed to die. That liberty can only continue in a secure relationship. A healthy couple needs two people secure enough to reveal themselves in order for their bond to remain strong.

If you are in a relationship and your thought about yourself is, "I can't tell him what I'm really feeling right now, because if I do, he'll think less of me; he won't love me." What do you do next with those feelings? You will start to cover them up and swallow your heart's need of expression. The temptation will be to start holding in that need in life that is not being met by your spouse. You hide it because if you let it go, if you reveal it – well, you just do not trust him enough. Your heart fears that the pain of hearing and seeing his response worse than the hurt of being alone in your isolation. Trouble is coming to your life as soon as that starts.

A relationship needs two people who are secure in their own personality and identity. They must be must confident enough to hear what the other thinks about them. That is often not fun because when your spouse says, "This is the way I'm feeling", that usually has some reflection upon you.

When my wife is feeling bad about something, there is usually a cause. As much as I would love to blame it on the kids all the time usually it has some reflection on me. I have to be confident enough in myself to hear her say how I have made her feel. Whenever she expresses some kind of concern about our relationship, my response to that cannot be irrational and heated. I must be able to look inward at myself.

If I am not able to do that when she points out one of my flaws, and I respond in a way to shut down that discussion, what do you think she is going to stop doing? She is going to stop talking. She is not going to be to expressing herself, and I will not either. When that happens, our relationship is about to fall apart.

Why do we think it is any different with God? True friendship, even with God, means that you are free to express yourself. You need to be free to communicate about what you are feeling. You need license to state what you are thinking about the other person.

Sometimes in relationships, what you are thinking about the other person is not good. You may not want to put voice to the confession, but your relationship to God is not immune from this dynamic. In the quietness of the night, in your own place of solitude, you have looked to God and said, "What are you doing? I do not understand. I do not believe it. How can I know?"

I would just as nearly guarantee that after those thoughts took root enough in your mind and sprouted just enough to break into consciousness that you felt worse for the experience. You felt weak for doubting God. You felt alone in your shame for doing something that is simply not supposed to be done.

Look to Abraham. He was in a strange land and had left his family behind. Abraham had given up everything in his former life all because God had told him, "I'm giving you a land and a child." Ten years later, he had neither, and he said, "God, what did I do in coming to Canaan? What are you going to give me?"

God says, "I understand. I am your shield. Nothing has changed Abraham. I told you before count the sand of the seashore. Count the stars of Heaven. Count them again, Abraham. The stars I made still decorate your nights. Count them again. The sand I ground from the rocks is still rough beneath your weary feet. Let its grains slip between your fingers. If you have any doubt, take these animals, I will bind myself in a covenant with you. I understand what you are feeling and I will do whatever I can to show you. I will tell you what I am planning. I will work it out for you."

In a true friendship, you are free to express whatever it is that is in your heart and mind. Open communication is the only path to friendship. The dearest friends that you have in your life are the ones that see you for what you are and love you anyway. God sees you for what you are. He already knows what is in your heart. You might as well go ahead and say it because you are not hiding it from Him.

Your fear of expressing your heart's doubt is only hurting one person – you. Because that fear to express what you are really feeling about the condition of your life is the very thing that will keep you apart from Him. God says, "Cast *all your care* upon me because I care for you" (1 Peter 5:7). He says, "Let *all your requests* be made known unto me" (Philippians 4:6).

The response to that is always the same: "Cast all your care, for I care." There is nothing that is going to be in the heart of a loving child of God that when it is expressed to God that is going to make God stop caring for that child. He says, "If you have something in your heart, tell me. Cast all your cares; not just the sanitary ones; not just the ones that have been washed and cleaned; and not just the ones that have been censored – cast *all* – for I care for you."

Those cares, doubts, and insecurities are no burden to God. Helping you find joy and fulfillment is why He created a relationship with you in the first place. Look at Luke 12:32: "Fear not, little flock, for it is your Father's good pleasure to give you the kingdom."

God's "good pleasure" is to give the kingdom to you. Think about what that means for a moment. Consider what kind of treasure the kingdom is and what it cost to give it. Giving you the kingdom meant giving His Son. Jesus suffered all of the horrors of His crucifixion because God's good pleasure was to give the kingdom to His children. The very treasure of Heaven, emptying Himself of the divine glory and taking on the form of a man and dying the death of a criminal on the cross was God's good pleasure for you.

What could you possibly have on your heart that your Friend would be too burdened to hear? What could possibly cost Him more than He has already given? Nothing. So tell Him.

You have something in your life right now that you want from God. There is something you are concerned about that you have been afraid to express to your God. You need to look to the cross and see the testimony of what He is willing to give for you.

The dream of a new best for which your heart is longing is not too grand for God. Your thoughts, concerns, and doubts are not too threatening to Him. They are His good pleasure. He stands ready and longing to help His friends.

Abraham was waiting for Isaac. Waiting and being patient is never easy. He needed to be to free to express his doubts and concerns. You are waiting to get through some trial, to get through this life, to reap your reward in Heaven, to see loved ones again, to see your children turn the corner . . . . . you are waiting. Waiting is always hard. While you are waiting, faithfully waiting, do not ever fear to express your doubt. The path we are walking down is not clear. We do not know the end of it or what is coming tomorrow. We are looking to move from the good to the best. Finding the best is never easy or clear. Our struggles to grow in our faith will usher unexpected concerns in our lives. Until we learn to express all of our hopes and fears and doubts that we have along that journey, we will never find friendship with God. Pledge, this day, to trust Him enough to be free to tell Him all that your faith needs to grow each day.

True friendship with God allows us to be free to express every doubt and feeling we have.

6

A DISTANT TORCH
TRUST YOUR FATHER
(GENESIS 15:12-21)

"I'll catch you."

Did you ever promise that to your child? Your daughter is perched atop a set of bunk beds or your son is standing at the edge of a swimming pool, and you make that promise: "Daddy will catch you." For some children, the promise is irrelevant. They were going to jump anyway. For the timid child, the scenario is an emotional storm.

That dilemma of trust was always clearest for me with my daughter. She was from her birth a "daddy's girl." As a child, she wanted my approval and attention at all times. Whenever I ever hugged her mother, her radar would activate, and she would come running to ensure that she received her share of affection. But that love does not remove the reality of fear. Placing her on a precarious perch and asking her to step off of it was fearful for her. In that moment, even a child understands the equation. Which is greater, fear or trust? If fear is stronger than trust, the child will remain in place, no matter the impact it has on her heart and the distance it creates. If trust is greater than fear, she will jump, no matter the height of the fall.

Trust is the foundation of every real friendship. You are friends with people because you believe in them. You believe in their character, abilities, and hearts. If every time they make a promise to you, you continually doubt or distrust that promise, there is not much of a friendship. One of the reasons that you may have distrust in somebody is because they may have failed you in the past. The limitations of our own human abilities, of our own insights, of our ability to communicate our desires and our intentions with one another fight against trusting each other.

With God that is different. There are different reasons why we have distrust or doubt. God has no limitations at all. There is no limitation in His communication or ability. He has no inadequacy in any of the areas that cause us to doubt each other. What He does have, though, is a perspective we do not. He may have plans that we do not understand because He has not revealed them to us yet.

In our first look at Genesis 15, we saw the crisis of trust for Abraham. He had reached the point where he had to have some further revelation from God to allow that trust to continue. God's plan, from Abraham's perspective, had been delayed for up to a decade (Genesis 16:3). In allaying Abraham's concern about the plans that God had for him, we can see some lessons for us about the areas of trust that we need to have in our relationship of God if we are truly to become the friends of God. We will see three different ways that our relationship with God must have trust within it. We have to learn to trust God in all hardships. We have to trust God at all times. We have to trust God that His plan is the best for all people.

God's Friends Trust His Plan in All Hardships

I wonder what leaving Ur must have felt like. We are not told what was in Abraham's mind on his journey. The best we can get is that passage in Hebrews 11 that says he was not thinking of the land that he had left behind (Hebrews 11:15). He had some commitment, maybe even hope, for the experiences in front of him. We discussed the ways that Abraham must have agreed with God about this calling back in chapter 2. We called it exchanging the good for the best. That action is almost always frightening, but it will not be taken without it also being hopeful.

Abraham Suffered Hardships

I cannot imagine a scenario in which Abraham would have had the expectation that by going with God from Ur to Canaan that his life would get worse. He is on a new journey. His God has called him to go on this great experience with him. How could this be anything other than the walk of a lifetime? Abraham's journey had to be a direct line to new and unimagined spiritual heights. Right?

And Abram took Sarai his wife, and Lot his brother's son, and all their possessions that they had gathered, and the people that they had acquired in Haran, and they set out to go to the land of Canaan. *When they came to the land of Canaan*, Abram passed through the land to the place at Shechem, to the oak of Moreh. At that time the Canaanites were in the land. *Then the LORD appeared to Abram* and said, "To your offspring I will give this land." So *he built there an altar to the LORD*, who had appeared to him. From there he moved to the hill country on the east of Bethel and pitched his tent, with Bethel on the west and Ai on the east. And there *he built an altar to the LORD* and called upon the name of the LORD. And Abram journeyed on, still going toward the Negeb. *Now there was a famine in the land.* So Abram went down to Egypt to sojourn there, for the famine was severe in the land. (Genesis 12:5-10)

Look what happens in those verses that describe Abraham's entrance into the land. God is still communing with him and continuing to reinforce His promise to His friend. On his part, Abraham is strong in his devotion to his Lord. He is stopping to build altars and worship his God at every place where he pitches his tent. When Abraham reaches the southern part of the Promised Land (the Negeb), he has walked the length of the great land that God has promised to him. No sooner than he has seen all that he had been called to receive, then the first crash of the waves of reality slams against the wall of his hope: "*Now there was a famine in the land.*"

Remember, Abraham came from Ur. We mentioned some of the wonderful and advanced abilities that were available in his homeland. The Sumerians were a wonderfully sophisticated culture. They were among the first cultures to master the art of irrigation. They dwelt in the deltas of the Tigris and Euphrates rivers. Those two important rivers brought life-giving water to his city continually. All of the life of the Fertile Crescent drained through their channels right through his home country. They did not have famines.

So, of course, the first crisis that strikes Canaan after Abraham arrives is a famine. If I am Abraham, I am having a talk with God: "Now hold on God, are you sure this is what you meant to happen? I did what you wanted, but now, I am suffering. My family is hungry and hurting."

His response is to flee down to Egypt. Does it go better for him down there?

> When Abram entered Egypt, the Egyptians saw that the woman was very beautiful. And when the princes of Pharaoh saw her, they praised her to Pharaoh. And the woman was taken into Pharaoh's house. (Genesis 12:14-15)

The first thing that happens to Abraham down there is that Pharaoh takes Sarah to be his wife. That circumstance would have done nothing to lessen his doubts about God's approval of the choices that he had been making.

After getting his wife back, he returned to the Promised Land. To be fair, he gathered some wealth (Genesis 12:16; 13:2). Yet even in that, there is the problem that arises within his own family that we discussed two chapters ago, "[A]nd there was strife between the herdsmen of Abram's livestock and the herdsmen of Lot's livestock. At that time the Canaanites and the Perizzites were dwelling in the land" (Genesis 13:7).

Because of the conflict, he is moved to give away his claim to the best part of what God had promised him. Surely now, the tide of trouble has passed. Abraham can have a moment of peace. No, there is yet another hurdle placed in front of him.

> Then the king of Sodom, the king of Gomorrah, the king of Admah, the king of Zeboiim, and the king of Bela (that is, Zoar) went out, and they joined battle in the Valley of Siddim with Chedorlaomer king of Elam, Tidal king of Goiim, Amraphel king of Shinar, and Arioch king of Ellasar, four kings against five. Now the Valley of Siddim was full of bitumen pits,

and as the kings of Sodom and Gomorrah fled, some fell into them, and the rest fled to the hill country. So the enemy took all the possessions of Sodom and Gomorrah, and all their provisions, and went their way. They also took Lot, the son of Abram's brother, who was dwelling in Sodom, and his possessions, and went their way. . . . When Abram heard that his kinsman had been taken captive, he led forth his trained men, born in his house, 318 of them, and went in pursuit as far as Dan. (Gen 14:8-14)

His family is entwined in the political conflicts of the day. There is a great battle among all the kings of the land. Lot and his family are taken captive. So what does Abraham have to do? He has to go to war to save his nephew. Again, if I am Abraham, I have questions in my mind. It would simply be natural to wonder where the blessings of the great land and nation are. Doubts would easily arise about the hope of the son that was promised to come to him. In the midst of these events, would you not lift your voice to God and ask, "When, God? When am I going to see the blessings you have promised?"

Going forward from the great encounter Abraham has with God in chapter 15, things do not necessarily get better for him. As we continue to study through his life, we will see further family troubles that he suffers with Sarah and Hagar (chapter 16). He will face challenges in witnessing the destruction of Sodom and Gomorrah (chapters 18-19). His son, Ishmael, will persecute the promised child, Isaac. Abraham will be forced to break apart his home and send his first-born child away with Hagar. Finally, in chapter 22, the greatest trial of all will come when he is commanded to sacrifice his beloved son to God. I cannot imagine this is exactly what Abraham imagined would happen to him on this great spiritual journey that he would take.

Abraham's Hardships Created Doubt

Even chapter 15, as God is promising that "I am still with you," look at what it says. In 15:14 as God is talking about the nations that populate the land in which Abraham is dwelling:

But I will bring judgment on the nation that they serve, and afterward they shall come out with great possessions. As for yourself, you shall go to your fathers in peace; you shall be buried in a good old age. And they shall come back here in the fourth generation, for the iniquity of the Amorites is not yet complete. (Genesis 15:14-16)

Maybe Abraham is just on a spiritual level that we will never know, but my mind would be filled with questions and even complaints at this point: "Wait a minute, God. Couldn't you have told me that before I left Ur? You brought me over here. I've been here nearly 10 years. I've been in war and in famine. My wife has been taken by another man. I've had fights and conflicts in my own family. And now you're telling me, God, 10 years later, now you're telling me that I'm not actually going to get the land. And my descendants are going to go down and serve a foreign king and be slaves for 400 years."

I have no problem placing Abraham's faith on a higher level than I have ever known. However, I do know that he was not immune from thoughts of doubt. I know he that would have the same kind of thoughts that we do because that is what is being expressed in Genesis 15. How else can the words of verse 2 be understood: "[W]hat will you give me, for *I continue childless*, and the heir of my house is Eliezer of Damascus?" (Genesis 15:2).

"For I continue childless" – there is more than a hint of impatience in those words. As we discussed in the last chapter, there is doubt in the plan. I have a hard time divorcing the hardships in his journey from that question that is plaguing his mind in this chapter.

Keep in mind that Abraham is having this struggle in his faith after having received multiple, direct revelations from God, telling him to come to the Promised Land. Can you imagine what Abraham might have thought if he had not had the direct revelation from God to go to the Promised Land? If he, on his own, thought he could serve God better in Canaan than in Ur and he picked up his family and moved to the Promised Land; can you imagine what he would have thought? Do you think he might have stopped at some point and said, "Maybe I shouldn't be here. I made a mistake in coming here. Is God trying to teach me something?"

The Danger of Optimistic Faith

Transitions in life can be invigorating and challenging all at once. How did you feel on the first day of high school or college, marriage or your job? I suppose there are people who are natively pessimistic who think "This is really going to be bad." Most of us are not that way. We go off to college thinking, "This is going to be the greatest thing in the world. I am finally on my own. It's going to be great." That first day of marriage, we dream, "This is going to be the happiest and most blessed decision I will ever make." The first day on the new job, we trust, "This is going to be amazing. It is going to be so much better than the last one."

In general, we are designed to be optimistic people. Every person who has taken out a loan on a car or gotten a mortgage is an optimist. Those acts are statements that we believe that, five, fifteen or thirty years off in the future, we will have an income equal or better than what we have now. The same holds true for getting married or having children. Those choices necessitate that we can believe in our prospects for the future. If we knew life was going to get progressively worse as time passed, we would not make investments in the future. That would not be rational, and most often, people do make rational, wise choices.

This optimism is even stronger when it comes to faith. The whole premise of Christianity is a statement of a better future. Our promise is that if we walk with God, there is an eternal kingdom and a heavenly glory that we get to share with Him. There is every reason to be filled with the power of the expectation of victory.

Yet, in that very thought much of the perplexity of the Christian life is found. The Bible proclaims that wonderful victory of His saints. We are more than conquerors (Romans 8:37). The One in us greater than the one that is in the world (1 John 4:4). We are kings and priests upon the earth (Revelation 5:10). Nevertheless, life seems so much less than that. Life is really hard, whether you are a Christian or not a Christian. The lives of both kinds of people experience the same reality. Your next-door neighbor may not be a Christian. The person in the cubicle beside you at work may not be a Christian. Does that matter? They work in the same place you do, in the cubicle next to yours. They probably make the same kind of money and live in the same sub-divisions. They drive the same kind of car. Their kids go to the same schools. They are going to have the same kind of retirement.

Their life looks a lot like yours. Day to day, in most ways, distinguishing between the saint and the sinner can be hard. Why is that? How has my Christian faith changed my life at all?

This conflict can cause us to begin to question the progress, or even the validity, of our faith. We start looking for the lessons in life that God is trying to teach us. We are fired or passed over at work; we get sick or have an accident; we are caught in up in a natural disaster or tragedy and starting looking for God's message in all of those things. We find punishment and God's discipline in the negative circumstances of our lives. In our troubles, we find God's dissatisfaction with us.

Most Christians I have come across take those things with humility. They endure them faithfully under the thought that God's way must be the best way for them. That attitude of humility toward God does not need a warning. The premise itself is what is flawed. The thought that God is teaching us things about our lives that go beyond the extent of His revelation – that somehow hardships or successes in life can be used independently of His revelation to direct our walk with God is not biblical.

Finding Certainty In Our Doubts

No physical or material outcome can invalidate a sound spiritual choice. Abraham would have been wrong to try to find God's approval in the material outcome of the spiritual choices he made. To obey God and go to Canaan was a spiritual choice. His spirit found agreement with God's spirit, and he went. All of the trouble enumerated in this chapter that came to him was simply a physical result. The famine did not make it wrong for him to live in Canaan. The conflict with Lot and the war to follow did not make his choice wrong. The judgment of Sodom and Gomorrah did not mean that God was unhappy that Abraham lived in the same land as those people. The barrenness of Sarah's womb and all of the trouble that came from that with Hagar and Ishmael was not a sign that Abraham should leave the land. All that mattered is what God had said. God's will, His plan, for Abraham's life was found in what God said, not in what happened to Abraham.

God did not intend His plan to change Abraham's physical circumstances. His plan had a spiritual goal. God's call of Abraham was not a method to insulate a man of God from trouble. In fact, it was an invitation to hardship, as we have seen. Those hardships were not a rebuke of Abraham. They were an endorsement of him. God knew that Abraham could take those steps, no matter how hard some of them were. Each obstacle he overcame in the Promised Land brought God's eternal plan to bring Jesus into the world one step closer to being a reality.

Hardships or successes did not reveal God's plan or His will to Abraham. God's word revealed it to him. What that word revealed was for Abraham to "go to the Promised Land." Until that revelation changed, or God added to it, Abraham had only one job – live in the Promised Land. Abraham needed to ignore any event that came as a result of obeying God's word. God's plan for his life was found in what God *said* to Abraham, not in what *happened* to him.

The lesson for us is no different and equally important. That perplexity of faith of which we have just spoken plagues Christians continually. We want answers to life's problems and to understand why the reality of our lives does not measure up to the expectations we have for people living with the promise of unrestrained heavenly blessings. Just as Abraham, we ask God, "What will you give me, for I continue . . ." We want to know what lessons we need to learn from God to receive His favor.

With our Bibles closed, we cannot answer the question, "What lesson is God trying to teach me?" The nature of His interaction with man has not changed since Abraham's day. Just as with Abraham, God still reveals His will through His word. When we try to use the events of our lives to interpret God's vision for us, our attempt to draw closer to Him has a real danger in pushing us farther from Him.

We cannot use the victories and failures of life to find God's will and end up in any place other than humanism. That is true even for people of faith that would vehemently denounce secular and humanistic philosophy. Without revelation from God on an action, all we have left is our hearts to guide us in the interpretation of the events that surround us. Even if those hearts have been well trained from Scripture, they are not perfect. The longer our hearts go seeking direction from events and not revelation, the farther they will get from the mind of God. Slowly, our hearts will begin to find validation in the things that make them happy, not the things that make them holy. We will end up with a standard of morality closer to the pragmatic humanist than to God. In time, our hearts will reject God. We will find in God an obstacle to our happiness.

Autonomous hearts will hear God's word calling them to avoid the things that make them happy. We will look back on our former, Christian lifestyle and be thankful we left it behind because we are more contented now. The life we are living now is easier and happier. Before we were bound by the rigid requirements of a black and white morality, but now when our hearts find themselves unhappy, hurting, or bored, we are free and justified to change everything about ourselves. If we pay any attention to God at all, we will say, "Surely, God would want me to be happy." If our hearts are happy and our circumstances are good then God must be pleased. If the opposite is true, then God must be just as despondent about our lives as our heart is. True, not every soul that seeks to find God's lessons in the events of its life will end up in that place. Most will not progress that far. The point is that place is at the end of the road for every soul that seeks to find God's will in events instead of revelation.

Sound spiritual principles will often benefit your life for the better, true. Yet that is not their primary purpose. Their intent is first to mold your spirit. They are intended to change your heart, not your life. The gospel trains your spirit to make sound spiritual choices. The Bible is not trying to reveal the specific, material choices that will be best for you to make.

God placed those choices within your hands.

- Did you get a direct revelation from God telling you, "You should go work for _____?" No, you did not.
- Did an angel appear and tell you, "You ought to marry _____?" No, he did not.
- Did you receive a vision in the night telling you, "You should live in _____?" No, you did not.

If you go to work for one company, or you marry that person, or you chose to live in this place or another, or whatever the choice of your life is and your decision does not turn out the way you wanted it to or were expecting it to, what are you to think? If the choice is not sinful, meaning it does not violate what God has told you in His revelation (the Bible), why do you have the impulse to ask, "Why is God punishing me? What is He trying to tell me?" We are not prophets and so cannot know the consequences of an action before we take it. We are in no position to evaluate a present circumstance in the light of any future consideration.

Sometimes life is just hard. Hardships in your life are not punishment. Life is just hard. Waking up in the morning is often all that it takes to let the trouble start flowing. Sometimes bad things just happen because other people are evil. Bad things happen just because you are unfortunate to be where you are. One morning, some people in New York City just got up and went to work. Some towers fell that day. Do you suppose there was some message from God that those people were more evil than anyone else was? No, they were people who just got up and went to work one morning. Do you think God was trying to tell the rest of their families, "You shouldn't have been working in New York. You shouldn't have been working for that financial institution."? No. Evil people did evil things, and so people suffered.

We need to understand and begin to learn to use our hardships, not as times to doubt our relationship to God, but to use those times as opportunities to refine that relationship. Every one of those kinds of events can turn you away from God or turn you closer to God. God is not punishing you when things go wrong. His plan is not weakened through your hardship. Those difficulties are opportunities to put the sound spiritual principles of the gospel to the test. Those moments are when faith is needed most.

Abraham was right to go and stay in Canaan. He was right to do so because that is what God said for him to do. Learning to overcome the hardship and remain loyal to his friend strengthened his trust in God. His endurance in spite of hardship brought him closer to friendship with God.

You are right to follow God's word. It is His will for your life. You will find His plan for you in His word. Do not allow hardships that come to cause you to doubt what you know to be right. Overcoming those hardships by making use of what He has told you that He wants from you brings you closer, every day, to being His friend.

God's Friends Trust His Plan at All Times

Hardships are not the only source of doubt we can have about God's plan for our lives. Abraham's faith is being tested not only by the trials he is facing in Canaan but also by the passage of time. God's plan for Abraham was not a short-term plan. Up to ten years had already passed in the land (Genesis 16:3). As we just saw in his vision, he is told he is going to die before the land is given. Those same verses say that it would be 400 years before even his descendants took possession of the land.

Do you think he was surprised to hear that? I cannot see how he would have known as he left Ur that he was embarking on a journey that would take 400 years to complete. The initial promise back in chapter 12 says nothing about that delay.

I struggle to place myself in his position. I guess there could have been revelation that we are not told about regarding the timing of God's promises, but that is nothing that could be proven. As far as we know, the first Abraham heard of this four-century delay was in the midst of the covenant-making ceremony of Genesis 15. In that thought my heart goes out to him. He had changed everything about his life. He did so as a man already advanced in years (He was about 75 when he left Ur.), only to find out the time of the promises was not to be his.

Now what is Abraham's choice? He has to accept it, does he not? That is, if he wants to remain on the side of God. If he wants to continue to grow in his relationship with God, he has to accept that there is no way that he is ever going to reach the fullness of what he was hoping to reach. When he left Ur, Hebrews 11 tells us, he was looking for a city whose foundation and builder was God.

On some level, Genesis 15 just told him, "Abraham, short of the grave, you're not going to get there."

Talk about a mid-life crisis. All these great plans, hopes, and aspirations of all the things he was going to accomplish in life, and he finally has the dawn of reality upon him which says, "I'm not going to get done everything I thought I was going to get done."

What is his choice then?

He had a choice to trust. He was being called to trust God's plan, no matter how long it took to be realized.

In the same way, God's plan for us lasts for a lifetime. Are you ever going to reach a point where there is nothing else you could learn, no other way in which you could grow, no other way in which you could serve? Every day of life is an opportunity to grow in friendship with God. The goal of the text at which we are looking in this chapter is not momentary. It is not something that can be reached and then laid down and placed aside. You are never going to reach a point where God is done with you.

Friendships are grown over time. Every meaningful relationship that you have in your life is grown over time. Friendship has to be that way. No matter how well you connect with somebody in a brief moment, that bond will fade quickly if not reinforced over time. The longer two souls remain in harmony the stronger the bond grows.

Too often, we get impatient with our relationship with God. We start looking for some kind of validation: "If I could just find some way of quantifying this relationship. If I could just find some way of knowing that I have arrived, I could get comfortable in it." Unfortunately, that is not the way it works. If you want to find friendship with God, you must remain patient in this journey. You must learn to accept where you are in it without becoming complacent.

Abraham's call at this place in his life meant he would have to be patient. In those verses in chapter 15, as God tells him, "This plan is going to take over four centuries to happen."

There is a reason Abraham could not get everything that he wanted to get.

God's Friends Trust His Plan is Best For Everyone

Abraham, while he is singularly important in the world at that time, is not the only person in the world. He did not go to the Promised Land and find it empty, did he? Go back to Genesis 15 for a second: "Then the LORD said to Abram, 'Know for certain that your offspring will be sojourners in a land that is not theirs and will be servants there, and they will be afflicted for four hundred years'" (Genesis 15:13).

Abraham's children will go down and be servants in Egypt for 400 years before they come out again. He will live in peace to a good old age and be buried and taken to his fathers. So, neither Abraham, nor his descendants will have the land for a long while yet.

Why God? Why can Abraham not have the land immediately?

God tells him: "And they shall come back here in the fourth generation, for the iniquity of the Amorites is not yet complete" (Gen 15:16).

God is telling Abraham, there is more to my plan than just you: "I've got a plan for you, Abraham, but I've got a plan for *them*, too. You are not the only person in this world. You are not the only person I care for. I am trying to work out my plan for them also."

The term, "Amorites," seems to be used in a generic sense for all of the nations that were occupying the land (Joshua 24:15; Judges 6:10). In order to give the land to Abraham, God had to take it away from the Amorites. That is just obvious. Abraham cannot have it until the people that are in it are taken out of it.

To take it away from the Amorites, something else had to happen. The thought is implicit in the verse. "Their iniquity is not yet full." Before the Amorites are removed, the mercy and the longsuffering of God had to be expended. He was still giving those people the opportunity to change, to repent, and turn. Until God was satisfied that He had given them a long enough space of repentance, God could not take that land from them. In His wisdom, that process was going to take another 400 years. Because God was concerned about all of His creation and not just Abraham, Abraham and his descendants had to wait.

Do we ever really think about that? "God, give me this blessing . . . this opportunity to serve you . . . this job . . . " You pray for a new ministry at your church to grow and bear fruit. You want to get this promotion or that transfer. The desire for all of those successes is wonderful. Let us say God blesses you, and you get the thing for which you have been praying. However, to give it to you, He has to take it away from somebody else. There is only one job. There is only one Promised Land. When He says, "Abraham, I am giving you the land," He is taking it away from everyone else in the world.

God's plan is not always about us. Yet, that is how we speak of it. Even in this chapter, we have spoken consistently of God's plan for Abraham and His plan for us. In reality, that is not exactly the right concept for it. The call of Abraham out of Ur was not God's plan for Abraham. It was simply, God's plan. God was not trying to bless Abraham, He was working out His eternal purpose that would one day be realized in Christ and His church (Ephesians 3:10-11). The Bible's description of Abraham's life is much more about Abraham's place in God's plan than it is about God's plan for Abraham.

Placing the same emphasis on God's plan in your life would be just as helpful. When we talk about "God's plan for us," it is easy to focus on the "us" part. We ought to be more concerned about our place in

God's plan than about His plan for us. Keeping that focus will help us to remember that God's plan interacts with other people in and out of our lives. We will find benefit in remembering that every opportunity we get is likely one that someone else did not get and vice versa.

We thank God when we get them: "God, thank you for giving me this job. Thank you for bringing this person into my life . . ." Do we blame Him when we do not get the opportunity? When your co-worker across the aisle receives the promotion and not you, if you believe that God is working in the intricate details of your life to that degree, then He is doing that for another was well. In His wisdom, the other person needed it more than you did. We must trust Him enough to understand that when another is being blessed it does not mean we are being punished. Do you trust Him?

That question is the one facing Abraham in Genesis 15. Abraham had seen that nation he was living in. He had seen how those people were living. He undoubtedly had seen their need for God. The same longsuffering God that patiently answered Abraham's questions of doubt was the same longsuffering God that was trying to work with those nations, trying to give those nations the opportunity to repent.

I believe Abraham understood that. He saw that. He had to. You must learn to begin to see the nature of the God you serve in order to appreciate the direction of His plan. Abraham does not rebel. He does not say, "God, those people don't deserve the chance. They do not deserve this land. God, what about me?" He was a man who was beginning to understand what God was trying to do. He was developing the ability to prosper and serve contentedly within His place in God's plan.

How did his developing friendship begin to impact Abraham's character? He was able to glorify God whether he got the land or whether he did not get the land. There was a great blessing coming through Abraham and it would bless all of his seed after him, but the message of this chapter is that he would not live to see it. All the hardships he had been suffering were just the beginning. There is more to come for his whole family. His response to that message was to glorify God.

Keep reading his life and you see that answer. He said, "I am going to serve my God, because I trust Him. I trust Him when times are hard, no matter how long it takes and I trust Him to do what is right, not only for me, but also for all of the people in this land." In the next few chapters, he understands this trust. He has a trust in God's plan and nature to do right for everyone: "Shall not the judge of all the earth do right?" (Genesis 18:25).

Our friendship with God should begin to impact us in that same way. We should learn to see how our life affects others. This journey of friendship will help us take our eyes off our own needs and learn to see things as God sees them. We will come to understand God is in control of these things. Our lives are not about ourselves. Whatever God's plan for our lives is, it is not about our personal benefit. We may benefit because of it, but that is not its focus. We may just as well suffer greatly because of it. Again, that will not be its focus. Your place in God's plan will be about accomplishing God's work, His will, and His glory.

In our calling along the path to friendship, even as we seek the best in our own lives, we need to learn to serve where we are. The desire to arrive at the best can make us impatient and intolerant of delays caused by others. Friendship means that we have learned to trust Him. We have learned to trust that we can serve Him no matter our circumstance – in the up's and the down's – no matter how long it takes. Our relationship with him is not based on outcome or on how well we perceive He is blessing us. An implicit trust that we have in His insight, ability, wisdom, faithfulness, and the sufficiency of His revelation is the only secure foundation upon which to base and evaluate our relationship with Him.

Is that the kind of relationship you have with Him or is your relationship based on how the events of your life are going? If it is the latter, you are not becoming His friend. You still see him as your master. You still serve seeking His approval. That is not friendship – it is servant hood. That kind of service is destined to struggle. The only way to remain constant in serving Him is to trust Him as a friend.

7

WALK BEFORE ME
ACCEPTING YOUR FATHER'S LOVE
(GENESIS 17:1-22)

"This God – his way is perfect . . .equipped me with strength and made my way blameless"
(Psalm 18:30-32)

Every church has a "James." James attended the church for which I preached in Atlanta. Over the many decades of his service to God, he had filled most every role one could in a church. He was a leader, preacher, and teacher for congregations he had served. His dedication to the Lord was beyond question. His heart was as golden and genuine as any man I have ever known.

And yes, there is a "but" coming. James was just one of those people that saw the world through a different filter than the rest of us. His personality was full of eccentricities. He talked a little too long. He stood a touch too close. Sometimes others' eyes would roll in a class when he made a comment and he would nearly always make a comment. Those comments meandered through the paths of his mind as they came out. They almost were never exactly on the point of the class or headed in the direction I was trying to take the discussion. However, if you listened long enough, there would always be a point in his message. James' point was usually a good one – often a very good one.

He was a student of God's word. He had put it into practice in his life for many, many years. The impact it had on his soul was among the first things you would learn about him. I loved James. The whole church did. His funeral, just a few months before I left that congregation, was among the best attended I ever saw there. Despite his oddities, those saints could not help but show their love for James. If you had known him, you would have loved him the same as we all did.

I have to confess, however, he drove me nuts. He made it difficult for me to preach on certain topics. I knew if I got close to those few, select choices, there would be a lingering conversation at the end of services. That conversation would be the same one we had about that topic the last time it had come up. We did not agree on them, and he wanted to talk about our differences. Every one of those conversations included the line from him, "Cancel, cancel, reject, reject." That was his plea about the things he was saying. James never wanted to exert undue influence. He was not trying to coerce me into another position. He just wanted to talk about God's word and express his thoughts. Still, having that same conversation, again and again and again for more than a decade was trying. He had heard all I had to say, and I had heard all he had to say. Most people would bring new arguments or a new approach or at least create a *Cliff's Notes* version of the discussion, but not James. Each time, he would start at square one and recite each step along the way until the end. Such thoroughness was just his way. James was a special man.

Betty knew that about her husband. She once told me: "When he corners you like that, just walk into the restroom." I laughed and replied, "Won't work. He'd just follow me in there." James would have. He would have stood right beside me and continued talking. He probably would have been oblivious to the changing of scenery.

As much as the church loved James, it loved Betty more, partly because of James and partly because of Betty. Betty is exactly what a godly Christian woman should aspire to be. She has served her Lord in as many ways as her husband did. A math teacher by trade, she has a mind as sharp as any. She could have done an infinite number of things in her life. She chose to be James' wife and God's servant. Betty is a refined and dignified woman. All of the social norms that eluded her husband, she uses them with grace and comfort.

The odd pairing often had people expressing their condolences to her over the years that I have known them. The words were most often wrapped in a coating of humor. I hope they were all intended in the good nature the light-heartedness of their expression suggested, although I am confident some of them were not. I never asked, but I imagine she tired of them at times. I know I would grow weary hearing those things about my spouse over time.

I would have never chosen to live with someone like James. The intensity of his personality would have annoyed me too much. He would have overwhelmed my patience. There would have been too many conflicts. Living with someone like him would have made me miserable.

Betty did choose that relationship. Without question, that choice made her happy. She chose to live with a man whose uniqueness could not be missed. Again, I never asked, but I know there were times when his choices had to be hard on her. She never let any frustration she might have felt be seen. You did not have to try to see the love between them. There was a commonality that transcended any of the difficulties his quirks brought into their lives (I am sure Betty had her own, his were just easier to see).

Love, Commitment or Loyalty?

"Love" is the wrong word for that transcending quality. At least, "love" as we commonly use it is the wrong word. Our usage is too transient and emotional. In our modern culture, "love" is too moved by the swings of affection that respond almost violently to the events within a relationship. "Commitment" would be closer. A commitment is an enduring thing, unchanged by the bad times or the good times. However, its connotation can be cold and detached. Honoring a commitment can almost seem like a burden to bear. Using such a comparison would be unfair to a relationship like James' and Betty's. Theirs was far too engaging and tender. Neither was bearing a burden.

"Loyalty" seems like a better fit. People are committed to things and actions. They are loyal to people and emotions. There is a difference. The gap is the difference between duty and empathy. I might stay in an unpleasant work environment because of a promise that I have made or the needs that I can meet through my employment. That is commitment, not loyalty. The motivation is about me, not the others involved. Duty and obligation are behind my actions. Loyalty engages my heart.

Fans of sports teams are loyal. They are invested in the successes and failures of the team. The dynamic is strange. Empathy with your teams' failures often draws you closer to it than do its successes. You see its struggles and weaknesses, and they simply make you love the team more. Your heart aches with the players when they lose. People will stay with teams for an entire lifetime, just hoping one day to be able to share in the joy of the victory of that one big win. No matter how many times they are let down, no matter how many heartbreaks they suffer, loyal fans just keep loving their team more and more deeply. How else can you explain the Chicago Cubs' having so many fans?

Loyalty is based on the trust of intention. The pureness of effort is why people love the underdog. We believe in the effort of the weak against the strong. We are lifted up by the purity of their struggle. Even when they lose, we love them more because we believe their hearts were pure and dedicated. Their victory or their result is not that which we deemed worthy. Their intention drew us to them. When we see integrity mixed with desire, we cannot help but be drawn to it.

I never felt the need to ask Betty why she loved James. The reason was clear. His actions were often odd, but his heart was always pure. A man whose actions were so often imperfect (from our perspective), had a love for his wife that was always perfect and pure. I suspect she did not love him in spite of his weaknesses. I am confident she loved him more because of them. Harsh critics may have been able to mock his choices, friends could chuckle at his oddities, but no one could ever question the pureness of his intention to love his wife. She was loyal to her underdog. She had good reason to be.

Is Wrath Better Than Love?

Accepting another person's love is often harder than accepting their wrath. Wrath, we understand. We deserve it for our insensitivity and callousness. Loyalty and love can make the shame we feel even deeper. Trusting another's heart so strongly defies belief.

"How can she love me after what I have done?"

That question can confound the mind and fill a heart with regret. Spread out over the years, the accumulation of one's failures in his treatment of a loved one can paralyze a heart and ruin a relationship. "How can she love," can so easily turn to "I am not worthy." If that feeling festers, turning away from that love is easier than embracing it.

However, if we can learn to accept that another is truly loyal to us, that same expanse of years creates a trust and comfort that frees the soul. When someone dear to us can see us for all that we are and are not, when they can live through our failures and the hurtful consequences that come from those bad choices and remain unfazed and even grow in their affections for us, that is one of the most powerful connections that a human can experience.

Every successful relationship has that strong bond at its heart. I believe that is where James was with Betty. I do not think he felt any need to hide himself from his wife. She had seen everything that he was and was not shocked or repulsed. He knew she accepted him and would never reject him. That security is something that we long to know. We long to have a fortress that strong to protect our hearts.

The lesson in Abraham's life that is before us in this chapter is a call to come to the security in that thought. God is loyal to us. God places Abraham in front of Him and begins with a powerful statement, "I am God Almighty." This is not a threat meant to humble Abraham to fear. God's words are a promise, an overcoming promise. God saw Abraham for who he was. He had seen all that Abraham had done over the last 25 years – the good and the bad. He saw how incomplete Abraham and his body were to accomplish what God needed to have done. None of that mattered. Abraham had stood with God. His heart and his intention toward God had remained pure. It was now God's turn to make a pledge to stand beside Abraham.

Genesis 17 is a pledge of loyalty. God pledges that He has accepted Abraham and still believed in him. He makes that same pledge to us. We just need to learn to accept it.

A Pledge of Loyalty

What is your favorite sports team? If you are a sports fan, you can answer that question with a single answer. The kind of loyalty we are trying to describe cannot be shared. Being a true fan of the New York Yankees *and* the Boston Red Sox or of Alabama *and* Auburn is impossible. Those groups are mutually exclusive to loyal fans.

To become truly invested in a team or a person, there has to be exclusivity attached to it. Such exclusivity must be expressed in some mutual way. Teams take the name of their cities or states. Those who are not near them are excluded from their fan base. At the same time, it draws those closest to them even closer. They are the privileged few that get to be fans. Fans buy clothing and wear the colors of their team. They are bound to only one team out of many. These pledges are more than mere commitments. They are made powerful in their mutual and equal promises. Fans share in the deepest despair and the heights of achievement. It is not "their" loss; it is "ours." "They" did not win the championship, "we" did.

The co-joined hearts enveloped in a loyal relationship are safeguarded. My continuance in the relationship is not predicated on my ability to produce results. I do not have to be the best husband in the world to satisfy my wife. I just have to be her husband. In a marriage of loyalty, she just needs to trust my intention. She just needs to know that my heart is pure and dedicated to her. My wife needs to know that I am loyal. If I am, then it is safe for her to be unguarded and to share herself with me. She trusts that I will never intentionally betray that gift of trust. I will share in her joys and sorrows just as much as she shares in mine. Her loyalty allows me to relax and love her out of joy and not fear. In the end, it makes me a better husband.

God is inviting us to experience the depth of His loyalty to us. As we have looked into Abraham's life, we have been witnessing the effect of that call. In chapter 17, I see a transition point in the relationship between God and Abraham. Before this point, Abraham is being trained and slowly brought along the path with God. Much of God's plan for him has remained shrouded from Abraham's vision. God has only pulled back the veil enough to let His servant know that his choices are still pleasing to God. After this chapter, God opens His mind to Abraham in ways that show trust and confidence in His companion. God is comfortable showing Abraham the fullness of His intentions: "The LORD said, 'Shall I hide from Abraham what I am about to do, seeing that Abraham shall surely become a great and mighty nation, and all the nations of the earth shall be blessed in him'" (Genesis 18:17-18).

What stands between the encounters at which we have already looked and the ones still to come is an encounter with God asking for a pledge of loyalty. Chapter 17 is about God and Abraham. Look at how often this chapter ties the two growing friends together:

- "[T]hat I may make my covenant between me and you" (v. 2).
- "Behold, my covenant is with you" (v. 4).
- "I will make you . . . I will make you" (v. 6).
- "I will establish my covenant between me and you" (v. 7).
- "I will give to you"(v. 8).
- "As for you, you shall keep my covenant" (v. 9).
- "This is my covenant, which you shall keep, between me and you" (v. 10).
- "[I]t shall be a sign of the covenant between me and you" (v. 11).
- "So shall my covenant be in your flesh" (v. 13).

God is pledging to bind himself to Abraham in a way that is unique among all the people of the earth. All that remains between Abraham and the fulfillment of what he has desired most – a son – is a pledge equal to the one that God is making. God is saying, "I will do all of this for you, but you must show that I am just as special to you. I need to know that you are loyal to me."

The evidence of that pledge of loyalty was circumcision. God created a sign of the covenant between Him and His unique friend and his offspring (17:11). Just as a spouse wears a special ring and fans wear their teams' colors, Abraham and his descendants would show the exclusivity of God's call on their lives. Circumcision would remind both Abraham and God of the pledge of loyalty enduring between them.

True loyalty needs more than just a token marking a body. Loyalty begins from within. The trust we have in another's intention is its foundation. Loyalty believes in the integrity of one's desire to what is right. That is true of fans and teams, husbands and wives, and God and man. Before the final promises of this chapter are extended and before God reveals the binding token of circumcision to Abraham, He needs to know that quality is truly within this man. This encounter begins with this command from God:

When Abram was ninety-nine years old the LORD appeared to Abram and said to him, "I am God Almighty; walk before me, and be blameless, that I may make my covenant between me and you, and may multiply you greatly. (Genesis 17:1-2)

Three statements are made with that command: 1) I am God Almighty; 2) walk before me; 3) be blameless. Two of them are about Abraham and what he must be. One of them is about what God is. All three of them are needed to understand the power of a relationship of loyalty with God.

Let's start by looking at what God needed from Abraham.

Walk Before Me

The command is simple: "Walk before me." What is it that God is requiring of Abraham? To answer that question, let us look at other times that same phrase (and similar ones) occurs in the Bible.

- Enoch walked with God after he fathered Methuselah 300 years and had other sons and daughters. Thus all the days of Enoch were 365 years. Enoch walked with God, and he was not, for God took him. (Genesis 5:22-24)
- These are the generations of Noah. Noah was a righteous man, blameless in his generation. Noah walked with God. (Genesis 6:9)
- And he blessed Joseph and said, "The God before whom my fathers Abraham and Isaac walked, the God who has been my shepherd all my life long to this day." (Genesis 48:15)
- That the LORD may establish his word that he spoke concerning me, saying, "If your sons pay close attention to their way, to walk before me in faithfulness with all their heart and with all their soul, you shall not lack a man on the throne of Israel." (1 Kings 2:4)
- And Solomon said, "You have shown great and steadfast love to your servant David my father, because he walked before you in faithfulness, in righteousness, and in uprightness of heart toward you. And you have kept for him this great and steadfast love and have given him a son to sit on his throne this day." (1 Kings 3:6)
- Now therefore, O LORD, God of Israel, keep for your servant David my father what you have promised him, saying, "You shall

not lack a man to sit before me on the throne of Israel, if only your sons pay close attention to their way, to walk before me as you have walked before me." (1Kings 8:25)

• "Now, O LORD, please remember how I have walked before you in faithfulness and with a whole heart, and have done what is good in your sight." And Hezekiah wept bitterly. (2Kings 20:3; cp. Isaiah 38:3)

• For you have delivered my soul from death, my eyes from tears, my feet from stumbling; I will walk before the LORD in the land of the living. I believed, even when I spoke, "I am greatly afflicted"; I said in my alarm, "All mankind are liars." (Psalm 116:8-11)

• He has told you, O man, what is good; and what does the LORD require of you but to do justice, and to love kindness, and to walk humbly with your God? (Micah 6:8)

First, look back through that list and see the characters that are said to have lived with that quality: Enoch, Noah, Abraham, Isaac, Joseph, David, and Hezekiah. The list is a catalog of the best and the greatest of God's servants. Whatever this concept is, it is clearly one that describes the people closest to God.

Second, examine the other words tied to this concept in those verses. Seeing the concepts closest to it is a great way to understand its meaning. Look at the following words tied to this concept in the verses above: *righteous, blameless, faithfulness, kindness, paying close attention, and whole-heartedness.*

Joseph's use of the phrase is interesting. In Genesis 48:15, he attributes this quality to his fathers, Abraham and Isaac and then adds that God had been his "Shepherd" through his life. One that walks before God has God as his Shepherd; the thoughts cannot be far removed from one another. The one walking is "faithful" to God and "pays close attention" to his heart and ways to ensure that he stays close to God. In return, God pays close attention to the well-being of this person just as a shepherd does for his sheep.

This concept is one of intimacy and harmony between God and man. Abraham had shown that with God. The call is an invitation for Abraham to remain close to God.

And be Blameless

The third part of the call to Abraham in this context is, "And be blameless." Older translations render it, "perfect." The command is strong, but it is also an equally strong promise.

The Hebrew word found in this verse is used about 90 times in the Old Testament. The most common use is in connection with the offerings that Israel was to make to God. Half of the verses in which this word occurs deal with the kind of animals that are to be used as sacrifices to God. Most translations use the word "blemish" to translate this word into English in these contexts:

Your lamb shall be without blemish, a male a year old. You may take it from the sheep or from the goats, and you shall keep it until the fourteenth day of this month, when the whole assembly of the congregation of Israel shall kill their lambs at twilight. (Exodus 12:5-6)

The word also has within it the concept of "wholeness" or "completeness." This concept is applied to things and periods of time:

- Then from the sacrifice of the peace offering he shall offer as a food offering to the LORD its fat; he shall remove the whole fat tail, cut off close to the backbone, and the fat that covers the entrails and all the fat that is on the entrails. (Leviticus 3:9)
- You shall count seven full weeks from the day after the Sabbath, from the day that you brought the sheaf of the wave offering. (Leviticus 23:15)
- If it is not redeemed within a full year, then the house in the walled city shall belong in perpetuity to the buyer, throughout his generations; it shall not be released in the jubilee. (Leviticus 25:30)
- And the sun stood still, and the moon stopped, until the nation took vengeance on their enemies. Is this not written in the Book of Jashar? The sun stopped in the midst of Heaven and did not hurry to set for about a whole day. (Joshua 10:13)
- If they say, "Come with us, let us lie in wait for blood; let us ambush the innocent without reason; like Sheol let us swallow them alive, and whole, like those who go down to the pit." (Proverbs 1:11-12)

The idea is that of a whole or complete heart toward God. This heart is fully focused on Him so that no part of it is spotted or blemished from turning away from Him. From that thought, in some verses it is translated as "blameless" or "perfect." The word is a way of expressing one's integrity or loyalty to God:

- Now therefore fear the LORD and serve him in sincerity and in faithfulness. Put away the gods that your fathers served beyond the River and in Egypt, and serve the LORD. (Joshua 24:14)
- I was blameless before him, and I kept myself from guilt. (2 Samuel 22:24)
- He who walks blamelessly and does what is right and speaks truth in his heart. (Psalm 15:2)
- I will ponder the way that is blameless. Oh when will you come to me? I will walk with integrity of heart within my house. (Psalm 101:2)
- Those of crooked heart are an abomination to the LORD, but those of blameless ways are his delight. (Proverbs 11:20)

Notice again the words associated with "blameless." The "blameless" are faithful, walk in the integrity of their hearts, speak truth, and do what is right. They are contrasted against those that are of "crooked heart."

There is no war raging within the soul of this kind of person. His affections belong only to God. Therefore, this person does exactly what God wants him to do:

- Blessed are those whose way is blameless, who walk in the law of the LORD! Blessed are those who keep his testimonies, who seek him with their whole heart, who also do no wrong, but walk in his ways! (Psalm 119:1-3)
- May my heart be blameless in your statutes, that I may not be put to shame! (Psalm 119:80)

This blameless one lives wholly under the direction and the control of God.

What is critical to understand here, especially in our study of friendship, is the motivation of this blameless condition. This obedience is that which is done with the whole heart and done in integrity. The communion with God that we have been trying to describe on every page of this book is summed up in this word.

Blamelessness demands obedience, yes. Strict, careful obedience is expressed in this word and also in the call to "walk before me." This kind of person would never think of disobeying God. There is, however, no hint of fear in any of those verses above. The thought is completely of companionship. The blameless heart is, above all else, a loyal heart.

In that thought, I believe we find the promise that goes beyond the simple imperative of "be perfect." God is not calling Abraham to do something that is impossible. The call to blamelessness or perfection is a call of opportunity. Abraham's efforts to walk before God with his whole-heart will inevitably lead to his being blameless before God.

That God views man as blameless is also clearly proclaimed in the use of this word in the Old Testament. One passage in particular stands out for our examination:

You shall be blameless before the LORD *your God, for these nations, which you are about to dispossess, listen to fortune-tellers and to diviners. But as for you, the* LORD *your God has not allowed you to do this.* (Deuteronomy 18:13-14)

When Abraham's descendants finally claimed the Promised Land, they had to drive out the Amorites that God had waited for during those 400 years. Part of the Amorites' sin was their reliance on the magicians and psychics of the day. God would not permit that among Israel. His people would listen to Him and Him alone. Interestingly, the next verse (v. 15) begins the prophecy about the great Prophet (Jesus) that God would send to His people one day.

God's work among His people, through His Law, called them to His side. The Law forbade them from turning to idols or the occult in any way at all. His commands compelled complete reliance on Him. In time, they would shape their hearts to follow Him and Him alone. A whole-hearted relationship is a life of integrity as it follows God. The whole point of God's law was to create people that were "blameless."

Jesus echoed these thoughts in answering the question, "What is the greatest commandment of the law?" "And he said to him, "You shall love the Lord your God with all your heart and with all your soul and with all your mind" (Matthew 22:37). The answer is, "Follow Him whole-heartedly." The answer is integrity and loyalty. God calls it "blameless."

The person who seeks God in this way is not only following the command to be blameless, he is living in the promise that he is blameless. God, who is loyal and full of integrity, has directed His servant's way to walk in loyal harmony with Him:

> This God – his way is perfect; the word of the LORD proves true; he is a shield for all those who take refuge in him. For who is God, but the LORD? And who is a rock, except our God? – the God who equipped me with strength and made my way blameless. (Psalm 18:30-32)

The All-Sufficient God

God's call for Abraham to walk before Him as blameless is a clear plea for Abraham to be loyal to Him. Loyalty was needed so that God could bless Abraham in the fullness of the covenant that He had promised His companion (17:2). The pledge of that loyalty was all that was lacking for those blessings to come. In this context, He makes one clear statement about Himself. He says, "I am God Almighty." The delay that Abraham had been facing in the coming of his son was not caused by anything on God's part. He is and had been the Almighty God. God is never lacking.

The Hebrew phrase God uses to describe Himself in this passage is "El Shaddai." In the Bible, this is the first occurrence of this term. We need to understand this word in order to understand the significance of this text. Scofield makes the following entry on Genesis 17:1:

> "Almighty God" (Hebrew, El Shaddai) (1) The etymological signification of Almighty God (El Shaddai) is both interesting and touching. God (El) signifies the "Strong One" (See Scofield) - (Gen_1:1). The qualifying word Shaddai is formed from the Hebrew word "shad," the breast, invariably used in Scripture for a woman's breast; for example (Gen_49:25); (Job_3:12) . . . Shaddai therefore means primarily "the breasted." God is "Shaddai," because He is the Nourisher, the

Strength-giver, and so, in a secondary sense, the Satisfier, who pours himself into believing lives. As a fretful, unsatisfied babe is not only strengthened and nourished from the mother's breast, but also is quieted, rested, satisfied, so El Shaddai is that name of God which sets Him forth as the Strength-giver and Satisfier of His people. It is on every account to be regretted that "Shaddai" was translated "Almighty." The primary name El or Elohim sufficiently signifies almightiness. "All-sufficient" would far better express both the Hebrew meaning and the characteristic use of the name in Scripture. (2) Almighty God (El Shaddai) not only enriches, but makes fruitful. This is nowhere better illustrated than in the first occurrence of the name (Gen_17:1-8). To a man ninety-nine years of age, and "as good as dead" (Heb_11:12). He said: "I am the Almighty God El Shaddai . . . I will . . . multiply thee exceedingly." (26)

God brings Abraham before him, and says, "I am the God-Almighty" or as the Hebrews' understood it, "I am the breasted-God, the supplier of nourishment. I am the place of satisfaction, of peace, quietness, and rest. I am the God who has all power sufficient to provide for you."

The name expresses another element of the pledge on God's part to remain loyal to Abraham. God is making a statement that He would provide everything that Abraham was going to need. He is saying, "I will be with you because you walk with me."

The Basis for Blessings

God is promising His loyalty to Abraham in exchange for Abraham's loyalty in return. God is willing to be the All-Sufficient God to Abraham in a way that is unique in all of His relationships with man. The basis for receiving the blessings of that promise is not Abraham's talents, intellect or any of his several abilities. The basis is the quality of his heart. He wants Abraham's whole heart.

Looking at a man of such unwavering faith as Abraham and never seeing any flaws is tempting. I think it is in part a defense mechanism we build into our faith. If men, like Abraham, are near-perfect, then I have good reason for not finding the same power in my faith as they had.

However, Abraham was far from perfect. We have already enumerated in previous chapters all of the challenges he had faced up to this point. Chapter 17 is specifically about the birth of his son, Isaac. Look again at the troubles he had there. At best, he grew impatient as he waited during the first ten years of his walk with God into Canaan. That pain was expressed in the question:

> But Abram said, "O Lord GOD, what will you give me, for I continue childless, and the heir of my house is Eliezer of Damascus?" And Abram said, "Behold, you have given me no offspring, and a member of my household will be my heir." (Genesis 15:2-3)

Perhaps as little as a few months later, he is working with Sarah to bring a child through Hagar:

> And Sarai said to Abram, "Behold now, the LORD has prevented me from bearing children. Go in to my servant; it may be that I shall obtain children by her." And Abram listened to the voice of Sarai. (Genesis 16:2)

His motivation was to help God in providing a son to him. That desire is good but is still not allowing God to complete His own work. I can come up with no reasoning for this action that does not suggest that Abraham's faith is at least being challenged. Yet again, the action itself is a statement that he does still believe that he will have an heir blessed by God.

Finally, even in the midst of the chapter we are discussing, as God gives to him the sign of circumcision, Abraham is still trying to work through Ishmael, Hagar's son:

> Then Abraham fell on his face and laughed and said to himself, "Shall a child be born to a man who is a hundred years old? Shall Sarah, who is ninety years old, bear a child?" And Abraham said to God, "Oh that Ishmael might live before you!" God said, "No, but Sarah your wife shall bear you a son, and you shall call his name Isaac. I will establish my covenant with him as an everlasting covenant for his offspring after him." (Genesis 17:17-19)

Abraham is not asking that God just bless Ishmael in addition to the promised son also as some commentators suggest. In response to Abraham, God promises to bless Ishmael greatly. He was to become the father of twelve princes (17:20). God has agreed to bless Ishmael. Yet, to Abraham's exact request that Ishmael would "live before you," the first word from God's mouth was "No!" Ishmael would be blessed, but he would not "live before" God.

At the very least, Abraham is asking that Ishmael be blessed equally with Isaac. The possibility exists, that even at this stage, Abraham is offering God another, easier path. His offer could be a request to use the son he already has, especially seeing that he and his wife are so old.

Still, however those words are to be understood, while they are less than perfect, they are not rebellious. Abraham still believes that God would bless him through his heir. That was always the case. Whether considering Eliezer, Ishmael or Isaac, Abraham never turned his heart away from God.

Abraham was far from perfect. His actions, at times, worked against the plan of God. His insights and understanding were equally misguided. Yet, his heart never left God. Abraham's desire never devolved into anything that could be called unbelief (Romans 4:19-20). He remained at all times loyal to his God.

On that basis, the blessings of chapter 17 come to Abraham. Abraham is bound to God on the basis of whole-heartedness, not performance. Was he occasionally weak? Yes, we have seen that. Was he limited in his abilities to accomplish what God wanted? Well, he was a 100-year old man, asked to father a child with a 90-year old woman. You tell me if he was limited. None of that mattered. He was loyal. God knew that. So God would bless him.

Friends Are Valued For Loyalty, Servants Must Perform

I know why Betty loved James. Her love was not conditioned on his performance. I am sure he did countless wonderful and kind things for Betty. I also know he did countless thoughtless and insensitive things. I saw her, many times, grading papers with her red pen before the start of Bible class. I never saw the school teacher keeping a ledger marked in that bright ink for her husband. His performance never received a grade.

We have an amazing ability to trust each other with our hearts. We admit how a husband and wife can find acceptance in each other's heart while knowing the limitations of the other's heart to act perfectly toward him. We understand how two friends can overlook each other's weaknesses to see the loyalty in their hearts.

Our struggle is to do the same with God. We cannot seem to process that God can view us in the same way that our friends and loved-ones do. The result is that we, for all practical purposes, hold a position that says our friends have a greater capacity to love us than God does.

Perhaps we have taken the Bible's call to holiness as a call to perfect living. Abraham was not called to perfect living. He was called to "whole-hearted" living. The difference in those two calls is infinite. One we can never live. I would guess, the other, you are already living. Most Christians I know are trying with their whole being to live for God. Yes, we take countless missteps alongside the countless good things we do. The limitation of our understanding and our abilities fail us at the worst of times. Yet, almost every child of God I know never gives up the fight of faith. Each time, we bind the shattered pieces of our hearts back together and move forward.

However, far too many of us take those missteps and project toward God our inner guilt and frustrations. We assign to Him the feelings of our own hearts about ourselves: "I am not worthy." In that action, we rob from our hearts the power of the faith that we see in Abraham's life. God never said we were not worthy.

Slaves are punished for failure. They are sold when they can no longer perform. Sons and friends are not. Abraham was not brought into such a dear place in the heart of God because he performed perfectly before God. The Bible says as much:

> For what does the Scripture say? "Abraham believed God, and it was counted to him as righteousness." Now to the one who works, his wages are not counted as a gift but as his due. And to the one who does not work but believes in him who justifies the ungodly, his faith is counted as righteousness, just as David also speaks of the blessing of the one to whom God counts righteousness apart from works: "Blessed are those whose lawless deeds are forgiven, and whose sins are covered; blessed

is the man against whom the Lord will not count his sin." (Romans 4:3-8)

Abraham's intimacy with God was created by faith not by the quality of his work. His tie to God was created because he was "blameless." His whole heart followed after God. Did that shape his works? Without question, it did. Abraham's works were numerous and most often, they were exactly what God wanted. Nevertheless, do not confuse the two thoughts. He was no lowly servant of God to be cast out as soon as his performance did not meet the quota. He was a son, moving to friendship. His worth was determined by his loyalty.

You share in that same pledge of loyalty as the seed of Abraham. So yes, work. Work and work hard for your God but not out of fear. God already trusts your intentions. He admires the qualities of your heart that have you seeking to walk with Him. Do not serve Him to gain His admiration. Serve Him because He already admires you. The step from that first thought of seeking approval to the second thought of trusting that you already have it, is the step from being a servant to being His child and ultimately His friend.

Learning to accept God's loyal oath of love is the biggest step in the faith of a Christian. Every time a Christian utters in prayer, "help us to walk in a manner worthy of . . ." or "help us to be better Christians . . ." I wonder if this message of God's approval of His people has reached his heart. There is nothing you need to do to be worthy of God's love. No grand act needs to fill your life to make God think that you are now "better" than you were before. Like it or not, accept it or reject it; God loves you. He will be loyal to you to the end. Living in the understanding of that one simple truth will transform your life.

You are Worthy of the Best

The power of faith is limitless. Becoming like God is your faith's aim. That goal is as infinite as the God who is its object. When we speak of "fulfilled" faith in this book, it is a bit of a misnomer. Faith can never be truly fulfilled. There will always be another place of growth for your faith. The only real limitation on how "full" your faith can become is your own view of your own worth before God.

There is an old hymn written by Frances R. Havergal that opens with the question, "Is it for me, dear Savior, thy glory and thy rest, for me so weak and sinful?" If ever the pain of unworthiness causes us to answer that question "No," our faith will cease to grow. In our moment of doubt, our ability and desire to exchange the good for another best is ruined. We will cease to believe that God will be willing to help us reach it. We will never see how God has welcomed us into His friendship any more clearly.

You cannot live a life that confuses your need of redemption because of sin with God's view of your worth and ever hope to find the best. Our only hope of seeing our true friendship with God is in learning the lesson of Genesis 17. We must learn to accept that God loves us and remains loyal to us. Accepting His love and trusting His pledge of loyalty to us will light the way to friendship with Him.

I was privileged to participate in James' funeral. Sharing in the intimate grief of a widow and church family was a great blessing. None of his quirks mattered in that moment. They were missed. What mattered in that moment was the memory of a pure heart. The memory of the impact of his loyalty was and remains powerful.

PART 4 - I AM GOD'S FRIEND

Friendship can only happen between peers. Only when both people in the relationship have a respect for the other's heart will friendship grow. No one would ever suggest that we can equal God in those ways. However, God does call us to be like Him in holiness (1 Peter 1:15-16). He does welcome us to partake in His nature (2 Peter 1:4). God has invited us to stand beside Him in a more intimate way than we may at first realize. God is mindful and respectful of man (Psalm 8:4). He has entrusted us to carry on His work in this world. He is willing to call His followers "friends."

> You are my friends if you do what I command you. No longer do I call you servants, for the servant does not know what his master is doing; but I have called you friends, for all that I have heard from my Father I have made known to you. (John 15:14-15)

In order to get to that point and see ourselves as friends of God, there must be a transformation in us that makes our hearts like His. We must begin to see the world around us and the people in it just as God does. Our premise is that "*Faith fulfilled ends in friendship.*" We are sons growing to be like our Father. His goal is for us to live just as Christ lived. God wants us to stand on our own – not without Him, but beside Him. He wants for us what every father wants for a son. He wants us to grow up and be men. Abraham is the prototype of that growth.

In Part 4, the last three appearances of God to Abraham highlight the impact that growth has had upon his soul. We will see Abraham challenging God's actions. He will be talking "man-to-man" with God. Theirs will be the conversation of two friends. That growing friendship reaches the pinnacle of its expression on Mt. Moriah over the prone body of Isaac. Faith has achieved the promise of its fulfillment. Abraham is fully God's friend. His success is calling us to follow.

8

BEING MERCIFUL
LOVING UNCONDITIONALLY
(GENESIS 18:1-33)

"And if not, I will know."
(Genesis 18:21)

By the time I sat down with Todd and Jennifer, the redness washing over the whites of their eyes was threatening to wipe it away completely. There was little reason to explain the pain the hardened lines on their faces was revealing. Sadly, their story is not that unique. What happened to them and their family occurs the world over every single day. However, the ubiquitous nature of the event does little to lessen the pain when it strikes your family.

Todd and Jennifer are wonderful people. They are just like millions of other couples trying to live their lives in a way which brings glory to God. They are the kind of people that a family and a church family can rely on for any need. Their happy marriage had born good fruit all over. Their children had grown up to love them and love the Lord. They had lived long enough to see those children reach adulthood, marry, and start families of their own. Everything was going according to plan and expectation.

From here, you can finish the story. One wrong choice of a son-in-law and the seams that held that family's happiness together began ripping apart. No father or mother raises his or her daughter to go through the pain of infidelity. In our world, we would be naive to think that betrayal cannot or will not happen to us. Nevertheless, that knowledge cannot prepare you for the shock. The touch of loss and helplessness one feels when the betrayal becomes known is horrifying to the spiritual mind. Their tears flowed freely as we talked.

They did so even for Todd. He is a man who was no stranger to carrying a weapon while on duty. Todd carries well all of the traits of strength and courage that go along with that burden. None of that strength could hold back his pain. This was his daughter who was hurting. She was precious and young and innocent. He was helpless to fix it and make his little girl better. So his tears joined his wife's in rolling freely down their faces.

We talked for a long while about their daughter. The three of us discussed what she was going through and what she might need or want from them. Walking the line between showing your confidence in your child's strength while wanting to make sure she knows that she can still find protection in her parents' arms is a challenge under such emotional stress. The whole conversation was accompanied by the unrestrained stream of wounded emotions. Their real pain is the only right way a parent, or any spiritual person, can respond to such a hurtful event.

Slowly, the conversation moved more directly toward the actions of the son-in-law. Like the light filling a dark room, anger lit their teary eyes. The response was palpable, guttural, and instinctive. I would have felt exactly as they did if I had been in their place. So would you. There is no excuse for what their son-in-law did. He deserves all of the hardship that comes into his life. Without the restraint of their conscience, those thoughts would have been voiced without regret.

We talked about him and his soul and how it needed to be saved. Our discussion moved to the cross and how Jesus had and would die for a man just like their son-in-law. I cannot go very long in moments like that without inserting the "Golden Rule" into the mix, and so we talked about it. Each step of the way, the mind and will of these godly people voiced their submission to God's word. Their emotions spoke with another voice. The fire in their eyes flashed in each unguarded moment and with each new thought. It was going to be a while, a long while, before they could interact with their son-in-law without the danger of that heated emotion getting the better of their self-control.

We all struggle in situations like that. Perhaps those whose hearts have been taught to know and respect the difference between right and wrong struggle with it more than others. The gospel teaches man about sin. It teaches him what man deserves when he strays from God. Our sensitivities are aroused when we see men seemingly living the life of the wicked, while seemingly dying the death of the righteous. Things are supposed to be just. Good is supposed to defeat evil. When those things do not occur, our hearts long to be vindicated.

In Genesis 18, Abraham is in that same place. Over the years of his journey, he has come to know a lot about the God he is following. The encounter of this chapter occurs the way it does because Abraham understands his God so well. He will voice his belief in the righteousness and justice of God. When God brings judgment on Sodom, Abraham's concern will be that God acts in a way that is consistent with the nature that he has come to know.

Nevertheless, this encounter over the fate of Sodom will reveal a blind-spot in Abraham's faith. Abraham will struggle to weave into his heart a love for even the wicked just as Todd and Jennifer did and as all of us do. This step is beyond understanding that we should care for the wicked to a willingness to do as much for them as we would do for our own. This loving quality is needed to sustain all relationships. Sooner or later, we will need to love someone who has done evil to us. Sooner or later, we will be the evil one that needs to be loved. Unqualified love such as this is a defining quality of God. The quality is uniquely divine. He is inviting His friends to learn this part of His nature.

Righteous and Justice – Two Out of Three Ain't Bad

Just before God executes His judgment against the cities of Sodom and Gomorrah, He makes this statement about Abraham:

The LORD said, "Shall I hide from Abraham what I am doing, since Abraham shall surely become a great and mighty nation, and all the nations of the earth shall be blessed in him? For I have known him, in order that he may command his children and his household after him, that they keep the way of the LORD to *do righteousness and justice*, that the LORD may bring to Abraham what He has spoken to him." (*New King James Version*, Genesis 18:17-19)

A few verses later, in the midst of their discussion about the fate of those cities, Abraham asks this poignant question of God:

> Far be it from You to do such a thing as this, to slay the righteous to death with the wicked, so that the righteous should be as the wicked; far be that from You! Shall not the *Judge of all the earth do right?* (New King James Version, Genesis 18:25)

Notice the highlighted portions of the verses above. They express something that God knows about Abraham and that, in turn, Abraham knows about God.

God says that He called and had known Abraham over all the years He had been working with him and equipped him to teach his children to do "righteousness and justice." You cannot teach others something that you do not first know yourself. God knew Abraham would teach those qualities to his children because over the last 25 years, He had trained Abraham to live with those qualities himself. Abraham had followed God with a righteous life. He had treated Lot in the same manner. God's man had treated the warring kings of the land in the same way. He had submitted to Melchizedek as a righteous man would. Maybe you could accuse Abraham of being unjust in his treatment of Pharaoh (Genesis 12) or Abimelech (Genesis 20), but those missteps are by no means a full testimony of his character. In nearly every example of his life, Abraham had "kept the way of the Lord." Righteousness and justice were at the core of his character.

Those same qualities are the ones to which Abraham appeals to move God to spare the righteous in Sodom and Gomorrah. Abraham knows that God is the judge over all the of the earth. He is the arbiter of justice. In that role, Abraham knows that God will do what is right. During that same time that God was working to equip him to teach righteousness and justice, Abraham was experiencing those same qualities in God. He knew that it was right for God to care for and protect the righteous.

In that sense, God's man knew that he was not special. God cared for Abraham in some unique ways because of the calling that the Lord had placed upon him. But this man of God also knew that he was not alone in being faithful to God. He knew that God always would do what was right and just. He knew that it was right and just to care for the righteous. Experience had taught him that righteousness and justice were at the core of God's character.

These two beings have come to know each other. They have a shared set of values. This chapter shows the confidence that each has in the other to live by the principles of righteous and justice – always.

Abraham Rebukes God

The scene of Genesis 18 is simply amazing. At least in Abraham's mind there is some measure of conflict between him and God over the fate of Sodom. God said:

> And the LORD said, "Because the cry of Sodom and Gomorrah is great, and because their sin is very grievous; I will go down now, and see whether they have done altogether according to the cry of it, which is come unto me; and if not, I will know." (Genesis 18:20-21)

Abraham heard in that statement that Sodom and Gomorrah were going to be destroyed. He had lived near them for two decades. He knew what they were like. He knew exactly what God would find down there. Those cities were doomed to suffer under God's judgment. Yet, Abraham knew there was a problem and was at least curious as to God's plans to handle it. Why else would he have immediately asked the following question: "And Abraham drew near, and said, *Wilt thou also destroy the righteous with the wicked?*" (Genesis 18:23).

Can you imagine the courage that it took for Abraham to stand before the God of Heaven and to say to him, "You shouldn't do that God"? That is the point of his question. He is concerned that God is going to do something that is not righteous. Abraham's conscience compels him to speak and begin that wonderful negotiation with God from fifty righteous people down to ten righteous. However, he is not unaware of the fragile ground beneath his feet. Each step along the way, in a variety of different phrases, Abraham says, "Now don't be angry with me God, but I want to ask one more question." And after that he says, "Again please don't be angry, but I've got just one more I need to ask you."

Could You Rebuke God?

How do you get to the point where you hear God declare His actions and have the courage to say, "No, God you cannot do that?" For some, that degree of forwardness is easy. The atheist says it because he believes no one is listening. The cynic says it because he thinks God is aloof or powerless to respond. Abraham is neither of those. He is God's chosen servant. He loves and respects God for His goodness. He respects His authority and power. How can one with such devotion to God question Him with such confidence?

The answer has already been given. Abraham is becoming a man spiritually. The son is growing into an adult. Abraham knows what is right and just from within his own judgments. God has taught him that. Abraham knows that God will do what is right and just. Shared, matured values based on truth give Abraham the confidence to speak. His mind is centered on the things that are at the center of God's mind. There is very little distance between their hearts.

The more important question than "How did he have the courage to speak?" is "How did he get that way?" How did Abraham become a person so in tune with righteousness and justice? How did he become so intimately and instinctively aware of the kind of judgments God would make?

That phrase back in Genesis 18:19, "For I have known him, in order that he may command his children . . . to do righteousness and justice," has the answer. The events of Abraham's life were not accidental. The appearances of God to him do have a purpose. Their purpose is growth. God is growing and training Abraham to become like Him. All of God's plans for Abraham were leading him to a point. Abraham became like God because God was teaching him to be that way.

All that Abraham needed to do was to follow Him in that "whole-hearted" manner we discussed in the last chapter. God would take care of the rest. By producing a mind that shared the same values as God's mind, the combination of a pure heart and God's teaching would transform Abraham over time. We have seen that every step along the way with Abraham. Every time there is a crisis or a challenge to the life of Abraham, who is there? God is there. Every one of these appearances from God in Abraham's life was a point of crisis – it was a point of change. Those times were crossroads where Abraham could have gone one direction or another. At each one of those points, God would come and His word would instruct Abraham to go where God would have him go. God never forced or coerced him to go that way. He pointed in the direction and waited for Abraham to follow. Every time that Abraham found one of those crossroads, he always walked down the path that God had taught him.

Your process is no different. Your process is the same effect of thousands of small steps taken with God's guidance. Unless you take the experiences of your life and see how they relate to the word of God, you cannot transform your life to be like His or learn to think like Him. You cannot have that kind of relationship with God that understands God's judgments as intimately as Abraham did until your mind is centered on the way His thoughts are. That unity of judgment will not happen until your mind has been trained to think the way He thinks. When God said to the Israelites:

> For my thoughts are not your thoughts, neither are your ways my ways, declares the LORD. For as the heavens are higher than the earth, so are my ways higher than your ways and my thoughts than your thoughts. (Isaiah 55:8-9)

He was not telling them that they could never think like He does. That is how I almost always hear people use that verse. Look at what He says in the verse just before it:

> Seek the LORD while he may be found; call upon him while he is near; let the wicked forsake his way, and the unrighteous man his thoughts; let him return to the LORD, that he may have compassion on him, and to our God, for he will abundantly pardon. (Isaiah 55:6-7)

His call is for the unrighteous man to change his thoughts. These verses are not saying that God's thoughts can never be your own. They are a rebuke of God's people for not having His thoughts as their own. Israel is being rebuked for not learning as much about their God as their father, Abraham, did. God's expectation of you is that you will learn to think like He does. Just as He trained Abraham to teach righteousness and justice, He is calling you to have the same kind of instinctive understanding.

This process is the step from sonship to friendship. A father trains a son his whole life in an attempt to ingrain on his heart certain values and principles by which the son will live once he steps out into the world. He does not want to have to answer the same questions over and over or to be forced to correct the basic behavior of a son who should be a man by now. Our heavenly Father is seeking this same transformation in us. God's aim is to transform us from immature, inexperienced children into His companions and fellow-workers with hearts full of shared values.

Genesis 18 is a test to see how far Abraham has come. God had brought Abraham to know what was right. The encounter of this chapter was an opportunity for Abraham to show and to see for himself just how much he had learned.

How did he do?

The First Step of Friendship – Faith In Action

Abraham has come a long way. In Genesis 18, we see Abraham acting in many ways just as God would have him to act. He does so without having to be told. Abraham's actions are instinctive and natural. There is a give and take in this chapter between God and Abraham – between two beings that shared so much and are beginning to see things through each others' eyes.

In the opening verses of this chapter, God appears to Abraham in the plains of Mamre. Mamre was one of the dwelling places of Abraham in the land. He has spent many of his days in that area of Canaan. That place was as close to "home" as Abraham has in the land. So when three travelers appear on the horizon, Abraham is placed in a position to serve as a host.

Abraham is in a time of communion with God and sees these individuals coming. He runs out of his tent to them and bows himself down to them and pleads with them to do him the honor of coming into his home. Abraham washes their feet as was the custom. He provides them a seat in the shade as would be expected of a gracious host. He provides food and water for them. The encounter begins with Abraham displaying his hospitality and care of strangers.

He does more than provide a snack of cheese and crackers for them. He makes bread from three "seahs" of flour (18:6). Three "seahs" of flour may have been around five gallons of flour and about 30-40 pounds in weight (Pfeiffer, Vos, and Rea 1793). Abraham humbly calls it just a "morsel" of bread. He kills a calf out of his herd and gives them curds and fresh milk. The size of the meal he placed before them would have been fit for a large American family's Thanksgiving.

In his dealings with these strangers, Abraham is also humble. As you look in 18:2-3, he bows himself to these individuals. He prostrates himself to them and refers to himself as their servant. In the early verses of this text, it is not clear if Abraham can tell that these beings might be divinely sent and perhaps even angelic. Perhaps in the appearance of God in verse 1, Abraham is told of the nature of approaching guests, but no one can know that. They obviously appeared in corporeal form because Abraham offered them food, and they ate it (18:8). Most commentators say that these individuals are angelic, heavenly beings. That is not taken from chapter 18, because they are not called that in Genesis 18. The connection is made in chapter 19. We believe that the two angels that arrive in Sodom are the same two beings that head there after leaving Abraham's presence (Genesis 18:16; 19:1). We will turn our attention to their time in Sodom in just a moment.

In either case, we know Abraham to be a man of humility that would show deference to God and His representatives and also his fellow man (cp. Genesis 23:7, 12). Humility is another quality in his life that showed he had learned the lessons of righteousness and justice.

Abraham is also a man of beneficence. Whatever these individuals need, be it comfort, food or security, Abraham was willing to provide it. He even goes so far as to lead them and to guide them. His guests were strangers in the land, and Abraham was willing to be their protection and guide. Abraham walks with them as they continue their journey down toward Sodom. His army of servants would have been feared in the land (Genesis 14:14-16). Any company walking under the protection of Abraham's presence would have been safe.

He is also, as we have seen, dealing with a God of loyalty. Abraham was that same man. God appears to Abraham in the early verses of this chapter and says, "I'm going to come back to you again in a year, Abraham, and you and Sarah are going to have a child." You need to keep that in the context of the overall study that we have been doing.

Remember that at the open of chapter 17, Abraham is 99 years old. He entered the Promised Land in his seventies. For 25-30 years, Abraham has been told, "The seed is coming, the seed is coming, the seed is coming. I'm going to make of you a great nation." Through the passage of thirty years Abraham has remained faithful. And through every day God has remained with Abraham.

Genesis 18 reveals a maturing relationship between God and Abraham. Abraham has grown in his faith. His mind is learning to think like God thinks. He is responding to people's needs just as God does. Abraham is righteous. That is beyond question. Abraham is just. That too is beyond question. His treatment of the three visitors in this chapter shows that he is living well with all of the qualities that come from those two traits. In his journey to grow from a servant to a son and beyond, he has done well.

But he is not finished.

The Missing Piece – Mercy

In this chapter, we have a different aspect of their relationship displayed between God and Abraham. The first five of the encounters involve God coming down and talking to Abraham. In them, God is directing Abraham and revealing truth to him. But in chapter 18, all of a sudden that one-way discussion becomes a dialogue. Abraham is asked to handle his relationship with God differently. The request would challenge his growth and will challenge ours in an important way.

There is something that intrigues me about this text. In a way, this is the most perplexing of the chapters in this series. I believe Abraham is still missing something. Abraham has learned of God's righteousness and justice. Yet, there is one more quality that he needs to see. What Abraham is missing in this discussion, in my estimation of this text, is an understanding of the mercy of God.

Abraham is Concerned for the Righteous

Let me see if I can point it out to you by asking this question: "Does Abraham have a righteous attitude toward Sodom?"

Abraham wants to do the right and just thing. His objection that he raises to God makes that clear. But what is the right thing? What is the just thing to do to Sodom?

Well again, that answer is pretty simple, is it not? As Abraham makes the argument, it is right for the righteous to live and the wicked to die. That is his argument: "Then Abraham drew near and said, 'Will you indeed sweep away the righteous with the wicked?'" (Genesis 18:23)

Note, Abraham's problem is not that the wicked are being swept away. He appears fine with God's determination to destroy the wicked. He had lived near them for many years. Had he been shocked at their immorality and idolatry? Had he received reports from Lot about the evil in the city? Had they cheated him in business? Who knows how those evil people had mistreated Abraham. Whatever his impression of them, he does not object to their destruction.

His question is, "Suppose there are fifty righteous within the city. Will you then sweep away the place and not spare it for the fifty righteous who are in it?" (Genesis 18:24)

See, Abraham is thinking, "If God destroys the city, He is going to destroy the righteous." If there are fifty righteous, God cannot destroy the city because God would kill the fifty righteous. That is Abraham's argument. Abraham's concern is that God not kill too many righteous people. That position seems so right and just.

God is Concerned for the Wicked

However, it is right here where my confusion exists. Abraham is concerned for the righteous. God is not concerned for the righteous in Sodom; He is focused on the wicked living there. I know it is an odd statement to make, but I think that it is true. Read this text with me again: "The LORD said, 'Shall I hide from Abraham what I am about to do?'" (Genesis 18:17).

God knows what is about to happen, does He not? Sure, He does. He is God. Now, what is it that He is about to do? He is about to destroy Sodom. Just read Genesis 19. Hold on to that thought for a moment.

Why do the angels leave Abraham and go to Sodom?

To answer that question, just look at where the angels go. They go to Lot's house. Their destination was not an accident. The angels enter Sodom for the purpose of going to Lot's house. Once they arrive at their destination, what do they do?

Genesis 19:12-22 provides the content of the message they delivered to Lot.

> [W]e are about to destroy this place, because the outcry against its people has become great before the LORD, and the LORD has sent us to destroy it. . . . As morning dawned, the angels urged Lot, saying, "Up! Take your wife and your two daughters who are here, lest you be swept away in the punishment of the city. . . . Escape for your life. Do not look back or stop anywhere in the valley. Escape to the hills, lest you be swept away."

In short, the message was, "Get out of Sodom!" The angels' job is to tell Lot how to get out of the city. Their message is, "Gather your family and your things and leave – now, and don't look back."

Given all that, I have a question for you: "When those men departed from Abraham and headed to the city of Sodom, did they have their mission already?" Of course, they did. The angels said as much to Lot. They did not say "might" destroy Sodom. They said, "We are about to destroy this place." The decision had already been made.

If their mission was to warn the righteous and they had that mission as they departed from Abraham, had God already provided for the righteous the way of escape? Yes, He had. God had already cared for and provided for the righteous. He did so by sending the angels to warn them.

Now back to chapter 18. Chronologically speaking, does the negotiation between God and Abraham over the fate of Sodom occur before or after the angels leave?

The men turn toward Sodom in 18:16 and leave Abraham's presence in verse 22. The conversation over Sodom's fate begins in verse 23. The angels were gone on their mission to warn the righteous in Sodom before Abraham ever opened his mouth in defense of that city. God's evaluation of the city of Sodom was not to determine the fate of the righteous. He already knew the fate of the righteous. Every righteous person in the city of Sodom was already prepared for or taken care of. Through the angels, God had already given every righteous person everything they needed not to be destroyed in Sodom. Abraham is right. God would not destroy the righteous with the wicked. He would not do that. Abraham's problem is that his vision is too limited to see a way that God can destroy the city without destroying the righteous.

God does not have that limitation. He had already solved the problem of the righteous. God was not coming down to earth for their benefit. Why is God there? Why did God come down?

Read his own words. In verse 21, God says to Abraham, "I will go down to see whether they have done *altogether* according to the outcry that has come to me. And *if not*, I will know" (Genesis 18:21).

There are two parts that stand out. The word, "altogether" and then the short phrase, "if not" are important. God was coming to make sure the wicked had done "altogether" what it seemed they had done. What was God's hope? "And if not," His desire is not "if" the wicked have or "when" the wicked have. His hope is that the wicked might "not" have done "altogether" as it seemed. The New Testament would say it this way, "God is not willing that any should perish. But that all men should come to repentance" (2 Peter 3:9).

There is something yet lacking in Abraham. God does not destroy the righteous with the wicked. He has already answered that concern. God had already solved the problem of the death of the righteous. God's concern was in finding a way to spare the wicked. Abraham never asked about the wicked.

Righteousness Precedes Mercy

Righteousness always precedes mercy. The concept and the understanding of doing what is right and being a person of integrity always precedes being a person of mercy. Mercy is the desire to not execute upon another the things that they deserve to have happen to them. The desire to excuse another from punishment without a firm and deep understanding of righteousness is always some mixture of apathy and weakness. Wickedness is overlooked habitually in our world. People are often exalted not in spite of their evil but because of it. Mercy does not exist there. There can be no expression of mercy when you do not believe another is truly worthy of punishment.

Establishing the worth of "right and wrong" in the heart of a child is among the first responsibilities of parents. I still believe "because I said so" is a completely valid reason to give a child. Before that child needs to understand why a parent is doing something, he must be trained to submit to his parent simply because it is right for him to do so. As a parent, I am not after a child's agreement. I want his obedience. He needs to learn that, "It is always right to do right. It is always wrong to do wrong. It is never right to do wrong and it is never wrong to do right" (Guess where I learned that.). After he has learned to submit his heart to authority, solely out of respect for that authority, he will be ready to learn the "why" behind right and wrong.

In taking that next step, there is often a struggle that a young person goes through. They are filled with black and white truths and are empty on experience. The young have not learned the true hardness of life. They have not seen how messy a person's life can become. Inexperience can lead them to a place of hyper-critical judgment. Parents, the people who taught them the great principles these young people now hold dear, are often the ones against whom their critique is first leveled. Has any parent been able to raise a teenager without being called unfair, a hypocrite, or a liar?

Looking back, I can see so clearly how it impacted me as a young preacher. I started preaching on a full-time basis right after graduating school. I knew so much. God's word was so simple and so clear. Understanding why people were not more energized to follow God's word eluded me. I was much like the young men John described: "I write to you, young men, because you are strong, and the word of God abides in you" (1 John 2:14). I was strong in the word and proclaimed it with unrestrained fervor. The result was that I grew to be far angrier than I had any right to be. There were sermons preached to (No, "at" would be a better word.) God's people that should have never been preached. Strangely, some of those sermons received the highest praise from church members. I guess I was not alone in my anger. I hope they will read this book. Like many young preachers, it was easy for me to equate faithfulness with attendance. Many of my sermons gravitated toward that topic. I am just glad no recordings exist of those sermons. The messages may not have said, "Come to every service or go to hell," but they often got close.

The problem with my early sermons' mentality is not the statement of the principle of righteousness. The actual point of teaching is right. If you are willfully neglectful of your responsibility to come together in worship or communion with God's people, you do need to repent of that.

The problem is in the unbalanced approach at the foundation of those sermons. If you exalt the principle of righteousness without the further development of mercy, you become self-righteous. You become hypocritical. One day you will be the person that needs mercy for sin. What then? You cannot admit your sin because you have already deemed that action worthy of judgment and impugned all of those who have done it before you. More likely, you will find a way to excuse it. You will justify it and will never come to God to find mercy. Your self-righteousness will ensure that you will never know God's mercy.

Righteousness - Mercy = Pharisaism

You become a Pharisee. Like them, you will profess an allegiance to God and His law, but you will miss the very heart of it. In a sense, they believed God was after "professional servants." Their traditional additions to God's law sought to keep man in a place where he would never violate it. In their own estimation, they were better at being His servants than any other group. The Pharisees' mentality was expressed in one of the parables of Jesus:

> Two men went up into the temple to pray, one a Pharisee and the other a tax collector. The Pharisee, standing by himself, prayed thus: "God, I thank you that I am not like other men, extortioners, unjust, adulterers, or even like this tax collector. I fast twice a week; I give tithes of all that I get." But the tax collector, standing far off, would not even lift up his eyes to Heaven, but beat his breast, saying, "God, be merciful to me, a sinner!" I tell you, this man went down to his house justified, rather than the other. For everyone who exalts himself will be humbled, but the one who humbles himself will be exalted. (Luke 18:10-14)

He was a "better" servant than the tax collector. He avoided all the wrong things and did all the right things more proficiently than his countryman. His basic premise was flawed. God is not after simple servants. He is not seeking to enslave man; He is seeking to transform him.

Learning God's righteousness and justice is necessary for the child of God. Any child of man or God must learn right and wrong. But there is more we are called to know. To the Pharisees, Jesus said:

> Those who are well have no need of a physician, but those who are sick. Go and learn what this means, "I desire mercy, and not sacrifice." For I came not to call the righteous, but sinners. (Matthew 9:12-13)

God came to make men holy, so that they could be merciful. He did not come to those who exalted righteousness and so their own ability to be righteous. He came to those who recognized their need for mercy so they would be able to give mercy to others. In so doing, they would become just like their God.

Righteousness + Mercy = God

Something strange happened over the years. I never changed my view about attending worship. You should attend. God commanded and expects you to come and worship with His people. If you did not go last week, go this week. What did change was my approach to exhorting people to come. People began to matter more. Worship was no longer a badge of faithfulness; it was communion with God and His people. Christians who chose not to come were not rebels and apostates from the faith but souls in need of help and encouragement.

It comes down to this. The older I get, the less I want to believe that evil lodges freely in the heart of others and especially in the hearts of God's saints. I know evil exists. I am not trying to ignore the presence of sin among God's people. I just know that life is hard. The people I know and with whom I worship are not evil. They are often tired and troubled or frail. All of us are from time to time.

Faith is strong, immeasurably strong, but it is also fragile. One unexpected assault from life, and it can come crashing down. Maybe I

144

have met one and just did not realize it, but I cannot think of a single child of God I have known that started His walk away from God on an intellectual level. I have met many that claimed it. They were deceiving themselves. Every time I have talked with them, there was always a point of pain. There was some deception or betrayal or isolation or just injury of life buried under all of their scientific reasoning. They may have become evil in their words and actions against the God they once loved, but they were not evil at the start. They were hurting. Their faith was weakened. Above all else, they needed mercy.

I suspect you have experienced the same feelings. You hear about some sister in Christ who has left the faith. She has done and said some hurtful things to her church family. You go to her and talk. As you listen, your heart is longing to hear some indication of an opening in her heart. You pray, "Surely, her heart cannot be that hardened. I have known her too long. This is not her heart."

How is that different than God with Sodom when He says, "I will go down to see whether they have done altogether according to the outcry that has come to me. And if not, I will know"? "If not," means, "maybe there is hope." Your compassion does not mean you have lost your commitment to what is righteous and just. That desire just means you are looking for some sliver of reason to believe in someone else for any basis at all to extend mercy.

Your impulse to show mercy means you are thinking like God.

If 10, why not 5? Or 1?

I have one last question for you: "Why did Abraham stop at ten righteous?"

His negotiations with God began at fifty. So he clearly believed that the death of fifty righteous would make the judgment on Sodom an unjust act from God. The same is true all the way down to ten righteous. Abraham's beliefs dictated that killing ten righteous in judging the city was an unrighteous act.

Why then, did he not ask about five? He knew Lot and his family were there. Going to five might save them. Going down to four certainly would because among Lot, his wife, and his daughters, there were four people spared in the judgment.

If five are worth saving, why not one? Why would Abraham not argue God all the way down to one righteous person? If it is unjust to sweep away fifty righteous with the wicked, if it is unjust to sweep away ten righteous with the wicked, why is not unjust to sweep away one righteous person with the wicked? More than that, why is it not worth at least asking God to spare the city for one righteous soul?

I can only imagine a couple of responses to that thought. The harshest evaluation of his motives of which I can conceive is that Abraham is worried about himself. Perhaps Abraham was truly worried that God would become angry with him and judge him and so he stopped at ten. But even in that harshest light, it reveals something about Abraham's thoughts. When the number under discussion is fifty, here are Abraham's words to God: "Far be that from you! Shall not the Judge of all the earth do what is just?" Those are strong words, indeed. Abraham believes that God is about to do a great evil. The evil is so great that God surely could not be angry at him for his objection. But here are his words regarding ten: "Oh let not the Lord be angry, and I will speak again but this once." Where is the anger over the injustice? As Abraham drops the number from fifty incrementally down to ten, his words become more cautious. His reasoning is clear. There is less injustice in destroying ten righteous souls than fifty righteous ones.

In the end, Abraham stops at ten, not because God has reached His limit. God has established His limit at one. Abraham stops negotiating with God because Abraham has reached his own limit. Abraham is satisfied with the number at ten. God's destroying fifty righteous is unthinkable, but it is acceptable that God would destroy one, and if He is questioned over it, He has the right to become angry at the querist. Abraham still has no idea that God is not going to sweep away even one righteous person. Abraham is indignant over fifty and complacent at ten and silent over the one.

His understanding of God's mercy fails right here. God would be indignant with even one of His righteous servants being swept away. He lost none in the flood. He lost none coming out of Egypt. He lost none in Jericho. He has never lost a righteous soul. God keeps working to deliver every soul He can find. He warns and waits to bring the flood. He looks and looks again to find the righteous in Sodom. His mercy is waiting for an opportunity to reach out to man: "Have I any pleasure at all that the wicked should die? saith the Lord GOD: and not that he should return from his ways, and live?" (Ezekiel 18:23). Abraham seems willing to exchange the death of a few righteous in order to judge the wicked. God will not do that.

I find it interesting that the Hebrew word for "mercy" first occurs in the Bible in Genesis 19:16 during the destruction of Sodom. Before this grand discussion with Abraham, God had never spoken of His merciful quality. Perhaps that is why Abraham is needing to see that quality of God in action. He knew righteousness and justice. But those paths alone lead to self-righteousness and ultimately entrap man in his own weaknesses. He needed to understand the quality that keeps hope alive – mercy.

In the last chapter, we explored a lesson on accepting love even as we recognize our own faults. This lesson needed to be next because they are so closely tied together. We have been given God's pledge of loyalty and love in our lives. To be and live like Him – to be His friends – we must extend that same pledge toward others. A pledge of loyalty only has power in the presence of mercy. When we have done no wrong, we feel worthy of other's devotion. Everyone is supposed to love a winner. Receiving a pledge in those times is expected. The true power of another's loyalty is coveted when people have fallen and are worthy of judgment.

If you are estranged from someone in your life right now, go back to them again. Go back and look again to see if his or her heart has "done altogether" what you think that it has. Maybe you will find the room for an "if not" with that soul. There is always time for judgment. But once judgment has come, there is no more time for mercy. Exhaust mercy's hope before passing it by.

God will judge, but He is quicker to offer and lingers longer over mercy. Abraham needed to learn mercy toward Sodom. Todd and Jennifer needed to show mercy to a flawed son-in-law. In order to have God's heart within us, we need to learn to show mercy to the wayward just like God has shown it to us. Without this quality, we can never hope to be His friends. Mercy is essential to His nature. Mercy must be just as integral to His friends.

9

CHOOSING ISAAC
KEEP ON GROWING
(GENESIS 21:1-14)

Live for the best. God will take care of the good.

Since 1980, there have been 187 seasons completed among NCAA football and basketball, Major League Baseball, the National Hockey League, the National Basketball Association, and the National Football League. In those 187 seasons only 95 different teams have managed to claim the championship of their leagues. Among those six leagues only around 20 percent of the total teams in them have managed to come out on top. If you are a fan of one of those teams that means there is some good news for you. If your team is good enough to win one title, it is likely good enough to win it again. In fact 46 of those teams have won at least two championships in that same span. American sports is truly a case of the "have's" against the "have not's."

You might expect then, with championship titles in major sports being shared so tightly among such a relatively few powerful teams, that there would be numerous examples of teams repeating as champion year after year. There are a few examples of it. In the NBA, the Los Angeles Lakers won three titles in row from 2000-2002. The Chicago Bulls matched that twice from 1991-1993 and 1996-1998. In the NHL, the New York Islanders won four in a row from 1980-1983.

In MLB, the New York Yankees won three titles in a row from 1998-2000.

Those extended runs of greatness are the exception and not the rule. In those 187 seasons, there are only 27 seasons in which the champion of the one season is the same as the champion in that league from the year earlier. Less than 15 percent of the time a team that wins a championship one year is able to defend that championship in the following season.

Why is it so hard to maintain success? You might look at several causes. In college sports, players graduate. In professional sports there is retirement and free-agency. All sports must deal with injury. Those causes are not sufficient. All teams in all leagues suffer through those things. Yet, championships keep falling into the hands of the few and not the many. Typically, good teams remain good, year after year. They just cannot remain better than those other good teams.

There is at least one other reason that needs to be considered: hunger. Teams that win championships are just not as motivated to do it again as teams that have not. Winning teams get rings, endorsement deals, and trips to Disney World and the White House. Successful players are rewarded with larger and larger contracts. Winning is good. The winners spend their time reaping the spoils of their victory. Competing teams spend their time looking at all the accolades falling on their rivals and long to supplant their peers at the pinnacle of achievement in their world.

The Danger of Success

Success can be more dangerous than failure. Hunger can be replaced with satisfaction, or worse, entitlement. Back in the opening chapters of this book, we discussed the concept of trading the "good" for the "better." We commented that at some point, each of us will struggle to keep making that exchange. Just like elite athletes, we can reach the pinnacle of our dreams. We go through the process of trading the "goods" of our lives for the promise of what is "better." If we do that often enough, we may just reach our "Super Bowl." We may just reach the height of our dreams. Having exchanged the good for the better over and over in our lives, we may find ourselves holding on to what we believe is the best.

How that impacts us will shape our relationship with God. Whether we keep pressing on or become content from our victories says a lot about us. Living larger than our dreams is dangerous to the human spirit. God has so wonderfully equipped and blessed us that it is possible to create a life in this world that is satisfying to us. Equating "satisfying" with "intended" is tempting. We can find ourselves in a place where we think, "This is where God wants me," because in that place we find meaning and happiness. Success can be as dangerous as failure. Complacency can rob you of your vision. When the good becomes the best our dreams can envision, we can become distracted and even entangled in the attachments we find in our good.

Abraham, What's Next?

I wonder what went through Abraham's mind the first time he held Isaac. There was his son. In his arms was the fulfillment of everything for which he had been living for more than a quarter of a century. The child was the fulfillment of God's promise to him. He had left behind his home, his country, his father, and family. Abraham had travelled with God into a strange land and endured all of the up's and down's that we have enumerated through this book. In his arms, he held God's best. Did he say, "Finally, I'm finished?" Did he think, "Now, I can rest?" I wonder if he thought his journey was winding down. Maybe he asked the scariest question of all: "What's next?"

Genesis 21 is God's answer to the question, "What's next?" The reply comes on a day that Abraham is throwing a feast to celebrate the growth of his promised son. Isaac is leaving the daily care of his mother to begin his training under the hand of his father. God had intended this for Abraham. He had wanted this man of faith to teach his son the way of the Lord in righteousness and justice (Genesis 18:19). There was another challenge in front of him. But Abraham is not ready to face that challenge. A hard choice still had to be made. Another better lies in front of him. In order to seize it, a good must first be stripped away.

Living in step with God is always a challenge. "No man can serve two masters" (Matthew 6:24) is the motto that stands above that way of life. God is singular in His purpose. His actions are never arbitrary or superfluous. He always does what is right and best. Being God's friend means living with that same purpose of character. You can never settle for the place where you are spiritually. God's dreams for His work in this world are more grand than your dreams can envision. Your hope in what could be must never become exhausted. When you settle down where you are spiritually, you place distance between yourself and God. God never stops working. When you stand still, He will keep walking. God always keeps working. His friends walk with Him to new dreams and challenges every day.

Taking those steps means that hard, life-changing choices must be made. Sometimes it hurts to leave the good behind because the good was truly good. Just as Abraham did, you will face this obstacle. With God's help, he overcame it. So can you.

Let's learn how.

The Best is God's Dream – Not Yours

A moment ago we asked how Abraham must have felt the first time he held Isaac. I wonder, how did he feel the first time he held Ishmael? At that point, he was around 86 years old. Approaching nine decades is a long time to wait for your first child. Do you think Abraham loved his son? I think he did. Abraham is not the kind of man that would capriciously reject a child that he was responsible for creating. On the day of Ishmael's birth, my mind's eye sees Abraham holding his first-born son with warmth, love, and hope for the future.

I may not be able to prove Abraham's love for Ishmael at his birth, but I can prove his feelings toward the his son at thirteen years of age. In the middle of chapter 17 as God is renewing his promise of Isaac's birth once again, Abraham makes this statement about Ishmael: "And Abraham said to God, 'Oh that Ishmael might live before you!'" (Genesis 17:18).

In an earlier chapter, we looked at just what Abraham is asking here. He is not making a small request of God. The phrase "live before you," is essentially the same relationship that God was pledging to Abraham when He is invited to "walk before him" (17:1). Abraham is not wanting his first-born son to be excluded from this special blessing. In his dreams, Isaac would come and be blessed by God but so would Ishmael.

Roll the clock forward a few years. Isaac is weaned, making him around three years old or so according to Hebrew custom (cp. 2 Chronicles 31:16). This would make Ishmael around 17 years of age. Abraham has prepared a feast for his son to celebrate this first step of growth. His son was ready to begin training under his hand. Isaac was starting his first day of kindergarten, so to speak. That is a time for the family to rejoice. In Abraham's mind, the whole family was to be gathered: Isaac, Sarah, himself, and Ishmael, too. Why should he have thought any differently? That was his family, and there was no reason to make any division in it.

Knowing all the thoughts in Abraham's mind at this point is impossible. But reading those first eight verses of Genesis 21, did you see any indication that Abraham is preparing to handle another great spiritual challenge? He could hardly be faulted if he thought that the work of his lifetime was winding down. He has done everything that God had ever asked of him. Three years have passed since Isaac was born, and there has been no further word from the Lord. Maybe, it is time to enjoy the journey to the best that God had in mind for him. Thirty years prior, God had told him the best was living in Canaan with his promised son. Abraham has it all now, or does he?

Funny thing about God – He never retires. He never gets to a place and stops just because it is comfortable or good enough. Sarah calls her husband an "old man" at the time of Isaac's birth (21:7). God does not care. God has plans for Abraham and his family that go far beyond any dream that Abraham could have ever imagined.

Seeing the "Best" in the Future is Hard

Have you ever noticed how few questions Abraham asked about the future? In the one chapter (Genesis 15) in which Abraham pointedly questions God's intentions about his coming son and the Promised Land, he asks, "O Lord GOD, what will you give me, for I continue childless . . . how am I to know that I shall possess it?" (15:2, 8). That is it. Abraham asks nothing about the 400 years. He does not ask which nation will enslave his descendants during that time. Never does he ask how his seed will bless all nations. God makes promise after promise about his family's future and Abraham hardly inquires past his life and that of his sons'.

153

Why is that? Abraham is no egotist. He is humble in all of his dealings with others. However, he is human. Pondering the life of your great-grandchildren and beyond is hard. It is almost impossible. He is like the rest of us. The urgency of life now and nearness of our concern for loved ones we can name is far greater than for those who are in the distant future. He is simply asking the questions that are nearest to his heart.

God is not human. His perspective is timeless and limitless. He is as much concerned about future generations as He is about Abraham and his family. Because of that, God is far from finished with this 100-year old man. Go back to chapter 18 again and read the words that God uses of Abraham:

> The LORD said, "Shall I hide from Abraham what I am about to do, seeing that Abraham shall surely become a great and mighty nation, and all the nations of the earth shall be blessed in him? For I have chosen him, that he may command his children and his household after him to keep the way of the LORD by doing righteousness and justice, so that the LORD may bring to Abraham what he has promised him." (Genesis 18:17-19)

God says those words to himself. The Bible records those words for us, so *we* know God's thoughts about Abraham. We might miss, however, that *Abraham* did not know God's thoughts. He never heard God say those things. God had chosen Abraham "that he may command his children and his household after him to keep the way of the LORD." I wonder if you had asked Abraham why he was in Canaan if that would have been the answer he would have given. Would his perspective still have been what it was in Genesis 15, "Behold, you have given me no offspring"? Abraham's focus, understandably, is on the birth of his son. God's focus is much farther down the road.

God's focus is ultimately on the Christ that would come through Abraham's seed: "And the Scripture, foreseeing that God would justify the Gentiles by faith, preached the gospel beforehand to Abraham, saying, 'In you shall all the nations be blessed'" (Galatians 3:8). From the first time God appeared to Abraham, His focus was on the gospel of Jesus. God's work in Abraham's life was never about the 25 years it took to bring Isaac into the world.

The best for Abraham's life was beyond his ability to imagine it. The best was God's dream, not Abraham's. This man of faith might have been content to grow old comfortably with Sarah, Isaac, and Ishmael. From every question he ever asked God in Scripture, from every plea the Bible tells us that he made for his family, that seemed to be his intention. He wanted to live before God with his whole family intact. In Genesis 21, his dream is complete. God's best is just beginning. There was more that Abraham needed to do to walk with God.

As we discussed the "good," the "better," and the "best" in an earlier chapter, we made the point that at some stage each of us would reach a place when we would pause in our walk to enjoy the good. Living by faith will take us through so many "goods." The power of faith to find the good, even in the midst of a harsh reality, is amazing. I see it in God's people every day. His blessings endure and allow us to find meaning and happiness each step along the journey with Him. Interpreting the good in our life as God's endorsement that we are doing exactly what He wants us to do is tempting. Doing so allows us to believe that we have achieved the aim of His plan for us. As soon as that happens, we settle down in our good.

The lesson of Genesis 21 is that our good is never the best. Even if we have been striving for 25 years to reach a place of service, once reached it is never the best. There is more for us to do. We may be able to live larger than our dreams, but we can never live larger than God's dreams. The best for us is found by never ceasing to unfold the layers of God's dreams as they touch our lives.

We need to learn to accept God's love of us no matter our performance for Him. We are sons and friends, not just servants. At the same time we must accept that there is always more that He is providing the opportunity to accomplish. Our inheritance in His house is limitless. Even at 100, God still needed Abraham to help prepare the way for Jesus to come into the world. No matter where you are, God still needs you to explore His dreams and find the best.

The time to leave the good behind is with us . . . again.

God Works Through the Best

Here's a recipe for a good time. Pick an important day on the calendar like Thanksgiving or Christmas. Fill your cozy three-bedroom home full of about 20 family members or so. Make sure each one of them has his own idea about what is going to go on that day. Mix in the fact that all of them are related, so they are comfortable saying whatever they need to say to each other when some kind of conflict arises. Then sit back and wait for someone to be the spark that gets the action started. Of course, this kind of setting has never gone wrong in my family. We are a group of loving, Christian people who love the Lord and each other. We never have any conflict. That is just like yours too, right?

Well, apparently Abraham was just not as good of a parent as we are. His family gathering did not go as smoothly. As the time of the feast arrived, his teenage son started to act up. Was he jealous over the attention that Isaac was getting? Did he feel truly like an unloved son in that moment? Whatever his issue, he began to mock Isaac. Sarah's response was immediate and harsh. She had already had a clash with Hagar over her pregnancy with Ishmael (Genesis 16:5-14). Apparently her discomfort or insecurity had not gone away. Her command to Abraham was direct and in my mind had just the tone that only a wife can make a husband hear: "So she said to Abraham, 'Cast out this slave woman with her son, for the son of this slave woman shall not be heir with my son Isaac'" (Genesis 21:10).

The feast was not starting as planned. The family discord hurt Abraham deeply. He loved both of his sons, and his heart is hurting over the prospect of losing his first-born (21:11).

The ability of small events to become life-changing is unexpected. This text is little more than a family squabble. Every family (except mine and yours, of course) has them. If it were not for the consequences of this fight, this story would not measure at all in the formative events in Abraham's great life. But God has different plans. Ishmael's immature action has opened the door for God to clear Abraham's life to bring in another best.

As Abraham ponders his next action, God makes His seventh appearance into his life. His message is one of agreement with Sarah, although His reasoning is far different:

But God said to Abraham, "Be not displeased because of the boy and because of your slave woman. Whatever Sarah says to you, do as she tells you, for through Isaac shall your offspring be named." (Genesis 21:12)

He says, "Listen to your wife." Hagar and Ishmael have to go. Sarah's reason is selfish and possessive, "the son of *this slave woman* shall not be heir with *my son* Isaac." God's reason for the breaking up of this family is a simple repetition of what He had said all along: "for through Isaac shall your offspring be named."

Sarah was right that Ishmael and Hagar had to go. She just did not know why and no one but God would have ever made the connection. Not until God inspired the apostle Paul to write the book of Galatians was this small family squabble elevated to a grand spiritual truth:

For it is written that Abraham had two sons, one by a slave woman and one by a free woman. But the son of the slave was born according to the flesh, while the son of the free woman was born through promise. Now this may be interpreted allegorically: these women are two covenants. One is from Mount Sinai, bearing children for slavery; she is Hagar. Now Hagar is Mount Sinai in Arabia; she corresponds to the present Jerusalem, for she is in slavery with her children. But the Jerusalem above is free, and she is our mother. For it is written, "Rejoice, O barren one who does not bear; break forth and cry aloud, you who are not in labor! For the children of the desolate one will be more than those of the one who has a husband." Now you, brothers, like Isaac, are children of promise. But just as at that time he who was born according to the flesh persecuted him who was born according to the Spirit, so also it is now. But what does the Scripture say? "Cast out the slave woman and her son, for the son of the slave woman shall not inherit with the son of the free woman." So, brothers, we are not children of the slave but of the free woman. (Galatians 4:22-31)

Sarah was right for all the wrong reasons. In her mind, this was about "this slave woman's son" and "her son." In God's mind, this was about two grand covenants of God: the Law of Moses and the Gospel of Jesus Christ. Man's mind was on the familial and the material. God's mind was on the eternal. Abraham was worried about his son. God was worried about all of humanity. Abraham saw the good. God saw the best.

God's vision of the best placed another crisis of faith in front of His friend. He was asking him to cast off one of his sons. I can hardly imagine the pain in Abraham's heart at that moment. How easy would it be for you, if God appeared to you and asked you do to the same? Could you just turn your back on your first-born child?

The Dilemma of the Good

There is the dilemma of the good. The good is good. A full, happy family is good because it is a worthy and admirable goal. In fact, a happy family is the main goal of many people's life. Finally, Abraham has it. But in one unforeseen instant, his family's happiness is gone like a ill-remembered dream. The good is to be cherished, loved, and held dear for as long as it is ours to hold. Letting go and reaching out for another best is never easy. But God's message is clear: "for through Isaac shall your offspring made named." God's work needs more than what is good.

God works through the best. Abraham's choice is right in front of him. Keep Ishmael and stay where you are or send Ishmael away. The first choice was a known quantity and good to have. The second choice would require Abraham to trust God to fill the void of Ishmael's departure with something more wonderful. Genesis 21:14 had to be hard for Abraham. As Hagar and Ishmael walked into the wilderness, they walked into an uncertain future. God had made promises about that future, as we will see in a moment, but the realization of those promises was now beyond Abraham's control. The good was being stripped away, so he could find God in the best. Abraham would have to trust his Friend to move forward.

Choose the best, and Galatians 4 can be written. If he makes himself uncomfortable in walking with God again, then countless millions of saints will be brought closer to God's heart as his spiritual seed. A new challenge was just around the corner. If he could have known what the next few pages of our Bibles had in store for him and his son, Isaac, I wonder if he would have been tempted to stay in the good. But he could not stand still and be God's friend. God's dream was not finished. To be a companion with God means fulfilling God's dreams, not his own. God's dreams are always found in the best.

The dynamic of your life is no different. God does not need you in the good. We might be more correct to say, "You don't need God in the good." That place is a place of comfort. Your faith is not challenged to grow in the good. You do not need to learn more about God to live there. What you have learned along the way has brought you to it. All you need to live in the good, you have already acquired. There is the problem. You cannot grow closer to God in a place of comfort. Jesus began the Beatitudes speaking of the "poor in spirit" for this reason. Until we feel helpless and inadequate to the task before us, we will not seek answers in God. The good is comfortable. However, our spirits are not impoverished there. Anyone can live in the good. That place of comfort does not transform you; it only rewards you. God is not needed to find happiness in the good. God does not want His friends to linger there. The challenge is that the path to the best is always uncomfortable.

God needs you in the best. You will not be called to expel your children from your house (no matter how much you may want to). That was Abraham's task, not yours. You will be called to strip away the comfortable places of service from time to time. Teaching the same Bible class for 20 years is good for you to have done, but is that the best that God has for you? It is good that you have finished school or raised your children or . . .

Are those things the best? This chapter is not for those struggling to hang on in their faith. This lesson is for those who have matured and walked with God into the Promised Land and gotten comfortable. You have forgotten the nervousness you felt all those years ago when you left your "Ur" behind. Your walk with God looks the same as it did last year or five years ago. There is more for you do to. Buried under the mountains of good that your life has produced is another best waiting for you. I know you love your "Ishmael." He has been a good son and filled your life with happiness. But it is time to send him away. Your best is found only in Isaac. Make the hard choice and find a fresh challenge of purpose in your life.

If your faith is not uncomfortable for you, you are living larger than your dreams. You are contented in the good. You need to see the danger in it. God's work in this world is all around you. He needs growing saints to seize those opportunities and fulfill His dreams. Each time you allow another pull of your conscience toward those dreams to pass you by, the distance between your spirit and God's increases. A comfortable faith can turn, unnoticed, into a dying faith. You are living larger than your dreams, but you are not living larger than God's dreams and they are the best there is for your life. God needs you in the best. Correction: You need God in the best.

God Will Care for the Good – Don't Give in to Fear

Abraham sent Ishmael away. He chose the best. God did not expect him to do that without a promise. As a part of His response to Sarah's command, read what God told Abraham: "And I will make a nation of the son of the slave woman also, because he is your offspring" (Genesis 21:13).

That was not the first time He had made that promise to Abraham. God made it in Genesis 16:10-12 and then again in Genesis 17:19-20. Ishmael's future was unknown, but it was safeguarded. Abraham was not abandoning the child to death (although he would struggle after leaving Abraham – 21:15-18). If he was listening to God's constant statement about Ishmael, he knew that what he was really doing was handing Ishmael over to God's care. God had a mission for Abraham that did not include Ishmael. However, Abraham's walk before God led to Ishmael's birth. The child would have never been in the world if God had never called Abraham out of Ur. God was obligated to care for the boy, and He acknowledged it. He had a plan for Ishmael. God never fails to have a plan.

Abraham might have held onto to Ishmael out of genuine, selfless concern about the child's future. He was wealthy and had a powerful army of servants in his house. Ishmael would have been safe under his roof for as long as Abraham lived. Once he left that house, those protections would be gone. One could understand if Abraham was fearful of letting him go. God was pointing Abraham away from Ishmael and down a path with just Isaac. Abraham needed to trust that meant that God would care for Ishmael. He would not leave Ishmael without protection. Not caring for the good is against God's nature.

Fear keeps us in the good. I do not mean by that just a selfish or insecure fear, although that would be true for some. I am talking of a fear for the state of the good we would be leaving behind. The same fear keeps us in the good that we know for far longer than it should. A church leader may stay in the same role year after year for fear of what might happen to a good congregation of God's people if he steps away. The same could be said for dozens of other roles in God's service. When things are good, there is always the fear that change will be for the worse.

Fear of change is a lack of faith that God will care for His own plans. Staying in a role for years on end because that role continues to challenge and invigorate is wonderful. The process of being challenged by an engaging work with God is exactly the process that presses us on to the best. However, it is another thing – for the worse – to hold on to a place of service that we know whose time has passed us by because we are fearful of the bad that might come. We need to walk with an absolute assurance in this thought: "God always has a plan to care for the good." If God is pointing you away through the pull of your conscience from the good, you need to trust that He already has a plan for what you will be leaving behind.

Back in chapter 3, we described a scenario in which a godly doctor might feel pulled away from a local practice to go work in a place where his skills would be more rare. Our point was that the doctor's pain of conscience was leading him a to new best. My encouragement to one in his place is to go. Go, and go now, if that is what your heart, trained by the gospel, is telling you to do. Overcome the obstacles and all the reasons trying to quiet the dream within your heart. One of the loudest of those contrarian voices would have to be, "What about all the patients I'm leaving behind?" That doctor, one whose heart is tender to the call of the gospel, undoubtedly would have been serving a group of people well. Those people would have loved him and needed him. He might be tempted to stay because leaving them would seem to hurt them. Fear is talking to you. Fear that I must stay in the good because I am needed there. That same fear would have kept Ishmael close to Abraham's side.

We must trust God. When we move from the good to a new best, the role that was our good is now open. God knows that. He has somebody ready. Someone will move to a new role. Your good will become their best. The exchange always happens that way. God will never fail to care for the good that you leave behind. His nature will not allow him to do anything else.

We cannot stay in the good out of fear. Understand, that when your heart calls you to a new best, your good is no longer your concern. God is not a corporation. There is no structure in place that holds back your "promotion" because all the slots are filled or that keeps you in a place because there is no one to take your place. Christianity and faith is not a business, it is a journey. You can take the next step in your journey whenever you are ready. Go ahead and take the next step of your heart. God has someone ready to step in behind you. I know you cannot see who that is. Being worried about the future is understandable. God has not called us to solve all of His problems. The problem that is keeping you from growing, He has already solved. He has called us to come learn of Him and become like Him. Problems belong to God. He blesses us with opportunities. The problems are His to solve, and He will solve them in His time and in His way. The opportunities are ours to seize.

Do not let the urgency of the good keep you away from the best. Your faith needs to be fulfilled. The call of your heart is leading you to it. God's call is leading you to friendship. Let go of the good. God is not there. He is in front of you, not behind you.

Sports teams find it hard to repeat as champions. Few teams are as hungry for their second Super Bowl win as they were for their first, and they have no "Superer Bowl" for which to play. We do. There is always a new challenge of faith to find. If your hunger is waning, that is your spirit longing for a new challenge. You are not tired or bored. You are starving for the best and just do not realize it. Along the way, you may have let your dream die. You may have missed as that dream slipped by you.

Time has not passed you by. Abraham was beyond 100 years old when this new phase of his life seized him. It is not too late to start again. Quit trying to repeat as champion of that which you have already conquered. Cast off the good and start over with a new best. You have a friend in God waiting for you in that new place of service. Now is the time for you to go join Him.

10

MY ONLY SON
UNDERSTANDING THE COST
(GENESIS 22:1-18)

"On the mount of the Lord it shall be provided."
(Genesis 22:14)

Just north of Adairsville, Georgia at mile marker 308 on I-75 there is a state-run rest area. There is little unique about the facility. The modest oasis has the usual vending machines and restrooms and travel guides that you will find in thousands of similar stops lining the interstates and highways of our country. People measure their visit there in minutes. As memory serves me, my family spent about three hours at this stop on the Saturday before Easter in 2008. Our stop was not by choice. Several years earlier either an engineer in the name of weight conservation or an accountant in the name of cost cutting chose to equip my wife's Volkswagen Jetta with a plastic impellor on its water pump. I am not exactly sure which of those is true, but I am leaning toward the accountant. Water pumps move a great deal of warm to hot coolant through an engine, and plastic has a tendency to get brittle over time. And so, about eleven o'clock on that early spring night, that impellor decided it was done doing its job. A flashing light on the dash informed us that our journey was going to be delayed. We managed to limp the vehicle into the convenient oasis provided by the tax dollars of Georgia's citizens.

The trip was not a vacation. I was scheduled to preach in Nashville on Easter morning. Our family schedule had dictated our late departure from Atlanta. That ensured our late-night breakdown would not be getting repaired before morning. My wife and I discussed our options briefly before I placed a phone call. Having read this far into this book, you know who I called. There was only one person close enough to me to help who would understand the urgency of my request. Shortly after eleven o'clock, Eric's phone began ringing.

My call came to him on a Saturday night. Eric had to preach back home in the morning. He was already asleep. My friend is a Marine and even years after his discharge still is much more likely to be awake before dawn than he is in the middle of the night. Over the years, I had suffered numerous early morning calls from him which stirred me from sleep, and I must admit that I did take a little joy in being able to return the favor this one time. What I did not take any joy in was the request that I was about to make.

It would be one thing to call and tell him that my family was stranded and needed his help. The drive was just about an hour and a half from where we lived. The trip was only a three-hour round circuit. Sure, there would be an inconvenience, but in our relationship, it would be a readily accepted request. No, I had a bigger favor to ask him. I did not need a return trip to Atlanta. I was expected to be preaching in Nashville in the morning. I did not need for him to pick me up. I needed for him to bring me a car in which to finish my trip with my family. That is a bigger favor. You see it involved rousing another member of his house and lending a vehicle to go on a lengthy trip. I was aware the request was a large one, but I never hesitated to ask it. I knew that and more was mine to have from him.

Around one o'clock in the morning, his two-car caravan arrived. I gained a new respect for his wisdom that night. He had woken his daughter to drive up with him, not his wife. He is a smart man. After a transfer of luggage and a hug and a big "thank you," my family and I were on our way to Nashville. I do not remember what I preached that morning. It was a long night.

Do you think after that night I felt like I "owed him one?" In most relationships, we do. When someone else does something nice for us, we feel an obligation to pay it back in some way. The dynamic of the relationship is connected to a give and take balance. Yet, that compulsion is absent in a true friendship. I never felt that way that night with Eric. I cannot remember the last time we kept track of who owes whom what. If we play golf or go out to lunch or engage in any activity, the money in my wallet is his and the money in his wallet is mine. There is just a communal approach to the entire relationship.

I do not know a single person outside of my family that I can truly say that about in every circumstance. The cost is too high to make that kind of commitment lightly. You will expose yourself to too much risk. As Solomon said, "A man of many companions may come to ruin." Friend is not a word to be used lightly.

We use that word far too commonly in our world. People who have just met call each other friends. Would they be willing to give away their time and money and possessions to help this new "friend"? I do not think so. The call at midnight would go unanswered. The cost of friendship is high. That spring night, it cost Eric a lot for such a simple thing as a broken down car. The request could have been much worse. There are so many horrific stories of life that happen to all of us. To be a friend means any and all of those stories are our stories at any unforeseen moment. Those pains are our pains. Friendship has great rewards, but the investment to receive those rewards is high and exhausting to maintain. Friendship must be chosen wisely.

The "Shirt Off Your Back" – Giving Without Sacrifice

Eric is among the most genuine and giving people I know. There is no doubt, in our relationship, he is the nice one. But even as giving as he is, the request I made of him that night is not something that he would do for everyone. He would do it for more people than I would, I am sure. He might do it for more people than you would. Even so, there is a limit. Not everyone in the world can get that response from him. Eric might come and give some a ride without trusting them with his car. He might find others a hotel in which to stay. He might help another find someone nearby to help them. There are limits to what we will do for others based on how close we are to them.

For some people, like my friend, the boundaries for those limits are expansive. We have a cliché for those kind of people. We call them "the shirt off my back" individuals. They are people that just seem to have a boundless supply of compassion for people in need. They are examples that we need to learn to emulate. The Bible honors that way of life and calls us to participate in it. If there is someone in need, what is our Christian response? We should be moved to help them. James said in this way:

> What good is it, my brothers, if someone says he has faith but does not have works? Can that faith save him? If a brother or sister is poorly clothed and lacking in daily food, and one of you says to them, "Go in peace, be warmed and filled," without giving them the things needed for the body, what good is that? So also faith by itself, if it does not have works, is dead. (James 2:14-17)

John said it this way:

> By this we know love, that he laid down his life for us, and we ought to lay down our lives for the brothers. But if anyone has the world's goods and sees his brother in need, yet closes his heart against him, how does God's love abide in him? Little children, let us not love in word or talk but in deed and in truth. (1 John 3:16-18)

Giving is the spirit of the gospel message. On a fundamental level, we should be willing to aid anybody that is suffering. If we are the people of God, we are bound to have that disposition toward other people. Yet, that attitude is not the thought about which we are talking. A bond like that with others is not friendship.

Think back a few years. Did you help out the victims of 9-11? Did you send supplies for those hit by the tsunami that devastated Indonesia? More recently, when earthquakes rocked Haiti and shook and flooded Japan, did your heart go out to those suffering such great loss? I surely hope you did. Giving would have been the Christian thing to do. James and John would expect at least that much from us.

The question is, "why?" What motivated you to want to help? Maybe you knew some people directly affected, but most did not. Millions of people sacrificed to help others in need and they had no direct connection to those people. For the Christian, the reason the lack of ties to the victims did not matter is our understanding of the connection we share in humanity from our common creation. God made us all, and He made us all in His image. The founders of this country were right in saying that "all men are created equal." In God's eyes, we most certainly are. Each of us is deserving of respect. The pitiable conditions each of those tragedies placed on innocent people were beneath the dignity of any man. Whether that man was good or evil, friend or enemy, loved one or stranger did not matter. They were people. People should be treated better than that.

I do not mean to cheapen the gifts that people made in the name of honoring another's humanity. Taken literally, when the clichéd "shirt off his back" man gives you the shirt off of his back, he is now shirtless. His gift has clothed you, made you warm, and restored your dignity. The gift is powerful and effectual. The offering brings glory to the name of the God that moved him to do it.

Abraham was that kind of person. When God called Abraham out of Ur, Abraham went. That is wonderful. But is the action unique? Given what we know about this man, what if Terah, his father, had come to Abraham and said, "Son, I need you to leave Ur." What if Sarah had said to Abraham, "We need to leave Ur." What do you think Abraham would have done? Is there any doubt in your mind that Abraham would have left at the needs of his father or wife? There is none in mine.

What about after he arrives in Canaan; was Lot the only person to whom he would have ceded a portion of his land? If there had been a conflict with one of the other kings in the land, Abraham would have been gracious to them. If another tribe or family was in need, he would not have turned them away. I would find it hard to believe that Abraham would suddenly grow possessive or selfish in that moment.

When war arose in the land and Abraham moved to save Lot, was his concern only for Lot? Did not he take those 318 servants and save not only Lot, but also the families and goods of all the kings? Yes, he did. The reason is simple. Abraham is the "shirt off his back" man. He instinctively responds to people in need. He should be praised for that spirit of giving.

Abraham gives without thought. Abraham gives to anyone in need. Abraham then, in a sense, gives without sacrifice. He does not possess these things so much and so dearly that he can't give them away. Abraham is a giving man. Nearly anyone, with a true need, could have moved Abraham out of Ur. Nearly anyone in true need could have received a portion of the Promised Land from him. If the need was great enough, Abraham would have risked his life to save nearly anyone that had been taken captive in war. God had trained His friend to give as naturally as He does.

Still, those gifts were not unique. When "the shirt off his back" man gives, his sacrifice says very little about his relationship with you. His actions say a great deal about his relationship with God and only through that, his view of you. That testimony is a good thing. The example should encourage us to be more like that man. We should give glory to God for his blessings because of this man's offering. However, we should not view the gift as some special sacrifice of friendship. Men like that would give to anyone in need.

Friendship Giving

That lonely night stranded on a Georgia highway, I knew what was coming. Even before the phone rang and stirred Eric from his blissful rest, I knew what he would do. I am his friend and that makes me special to him. He will do things for me that he will not do for you. There is simply a difference in the level of investment you have in a friend as opposed to a stranger. There is a different limit that is imposed on the claim that each person can make on our hearts. There is a great divide between *friendship giving* and charity.

Friendship giving is easily illustrated. If a stranger walks up to you and says, "I'm hungry. Can you spare a couple of dollars so I can go get some food?" You would almost certainly give him either the money or the food. You would probably do so with little thought about it. Providing for his need would simply be the right thing to do.

Then the stranger says, "I don't have a coat; can you buy me a coat?" Are you willing do it? The answer is still likely, "yes." The cost to you is higher, but every man deserves not to be cold. Meeting his request is even close to the very example of doing good that Jesus used in His time on the earth (Matthew 5:40).

Later, the stranger makes another request, "I cannot get around. I need some transportation. Can I have your car?" The cost to you has escalated. You had money for his food without your family going hungry. You had money for a coat, without your children going cold in the winter. You have two cars, but your family does use both of them. Do you give one away? Some would. I have seen it done. Do you stop and think for a minute longer than over the purchase of combo meal at McDonalds? Probably, you do.

Still another request comes. A stranger says, "I don't have a place to live. Can I have your home?" Is that your limit? At some point, this persistent stranger is going to reach yours. You might give your home away to some in need. The suggestion is not that you would not or that somehow that act goes beyond the call of the gospel or people's ability to sacrifice. But are there people in your life for whom that request is more likely to be granted than for others? Of course there are.

The giving that we are willing to do for friends is more intimate and special than it is for strangers. Read again Solomon's words: "A man of many companions may come to ruin." If you open your heart too easily to too many people, this kind of giving can bankrupt you emotionally and materially. Friendship can only be maintained among peers. The cost is too high for the relationship to work any other way.

What if I were unwillingly to give back to Eric or suddenly stopped, and he continued to give? We would no longer be peers. I would not be supplying anything back to meet his needs. Friendship would devolve into charity. If Eric failed to realize the change, his lack of discernment would have him falling into the grips of Solomon's warning. He would come to ruin by offering friendship to one that has not given it in return.

Only in the bond of friendship can truly unique and sacrificial giving be done. God recognizes the need of this security as we give of ourselves to others. We know that we should give to all men in need, but that gift of goodness is intensified with the family of God: "So then, as we have opportunity, let us do good to everyone, and especially to those who are of the household of faith" (Galatians 6:10). We can afford to be unguarded with our friends in Christ because of our common bond and purpose. This truth is powerful within the intimacy of marriage: "Let marriage be held in honor among all, and let the marriage bed be undefiled" (Hebrews 13:4). Marriage, at its best, allows for unrestrained giving of self and belongings to another. In it is the height of human friendship. As much as Eric will give to me, he would give his wife infinitely more. In the bond of true friendship, there is no need for protection. Sacrifice can be made without fear – even the ultimate sacrifice.

Abraham is God's Friend

We have reached the final appearance of God in Abraham's life. In this encounter, God finishes the purpose that He had for Abraham's faith. This special lesson should fill our hearts with hope about how God views our potential to walk with Him, but let's review the verses which speak of this encounter before we draw out that lesson.

In Genesis 15:6, the Bible reads, "And he believed the LORD, and he counted it to him as righteousness." That text gives us the basis of Abraham's relationship with God. Paul quotes those words in Romans 4:3 as the foundation of his argument that all men are saved by faith.

Yet, that passage is prophetic in nature. The faith that is in Genesis 15 is not complete or matured. His faith still needs to be grown. It still needs fulfillment. All along, we have held that faith finds it completion, its fulfillment in friendship with God. That thought is largely taken from James's use of Abraham's life. His discussion of these events reads this way:

> Was not Abraham our father justified by works *when he offered up his son Isaac on the altar?* You see that faith was active along with his works, and faith was completed by his works; *and the Scripture was fulfilled that says, "Abraham believed God, and it was counted to him as righteousness"* – and he was called a friend of God. (James 2:21-23)

Notice the two emphasized portions of James's words. The Scripture which spoke of Abraham's faith in God was not fulfilled in Genesis 15 when it was said. The scripture was fulfilled when his faith moved him to work and offer up his son Isaac on the altar.

Notice further, the connection between the fulfillment of the Scripture and his friendship with God. James looks to Abraham's life and brings Genesis 15 together with Genesis 22 and says at the fulfillment of the faith described in Abraham's life he was then ready to be called the friend of God. The order here is important. Not until faith had moved him to deliver his son to God was he fit to be God's friend. The offer of Isaac is special to Abraham's faith. Something that goes beyond just leaving Ur or sharing the land or waiting for a son to be born or even sending away Ishmael. This chapter is unique in the development of his faith. God's actions called Abraham to do something that even God understood as powerful and life-changing.

Isaac: The Cost of Friendship

James ties Abraham's preparation for friendship to the sacrifice of Isaac. So, how does the offering up of Isaac make Abraham ready to be God's friend? That really is the crux of the whole issue. I want to be with God like Abraham was. God wants me to be there. I know that because God holds Abraham up as the father of all the faithful. Short of Christ, his example is the one example of faith that we are called to follow. Understanding the dynamic of Isaac's sacrifice is critical to understanding the path to intimate friendship with God.

In order to see that connection, it is helpful to notice the way God refers to Isaac twice in Genesis 22. In the first call to Abraham God says, "Take your son." That would have been sufficient. Since Ishmael has been gone for many years, Abraham has only one son to consider.

God goes on, "your only son, Isaac." Again, that would be sufficient. In fact, it is beginning to be redundant. God is never redundant. He speaks no idle or wasted words. There was a point to the clarity of His address.

He is still not done, "whom you love." The whole call reads as follows: "Take your son, your only son, Isaac, whom you love." What is God trying to say?

God knows how special Isaac is. He knows that not everyone can have Isaac. In fact, I would guess that no one could. No man could come and ask for the life of Isaac and get Abraham to yield to the petition. God knows the gift He is asking has a high cost for Abraham. He knew it would be a test of Abraham's faith (22:1). His understanding is clear in the way He frames the command to Abraham. He knows this request has a much higher cost than anything He has ever asked before. Homes left behind can be replaced. Land can be reacquired. Family left back at home are not dead and gone. Everything God has asked of Abraham in thirty years, one can imagine that Abraham would have done for others in God's name. However, what He is asking now is patently different. God does not downplay that fact.

The word "now," in verse 12 is powerful in its significance:

> He said, "Do not lay your hand on the boy or do anything to him, for *now* I know that you fear God, seeing you have not withheld your son, your only son, from me."

As Abraham's hand is moving to take the life of his son, God stops him and says, "Now I know." Do not read through that phrase and not stop to catch the importance of the thought. What is it that God has learned about Abraham in the sacrifice of Isaac? He says, "Now I know that *you fear God.*"

What? Abraham has been walking with God for at least the last thirty years. Over and over and over, we have seen the faithful steps of this man of faith in his service. Way back in chapter 15, God said that Abraham had believed Him (15:6). Yet, not until this moment does God say that He knows that Abraham fears Him. What exactly does that mean?

Look at the usage of that phrase in Psalm 22:22-23:

> I will tell of your name to *my brothers*; in the midst of the congregation I will praise you: You *who fear the* LORD, praise him! All you offspring of Jacob, glorify him, and stand in awe of him, all you offspring of Israel!

Those that "fear the Lord" are His brethren. The passage is quoted and applied to the Christ's view of His humanity in Hebrews 2:12. The phrase is descriptive of those that praise God and stand in awe of Him. In other words, the one that "fears God" is a worshipper of God, one that glorifies Him and praises Him.

How does that help? Not until Genesis 22 does God know that Abraham worships Him and gives Him respect. Has God not been paying attention to Abraham's life? Those statements are made about this man from Genesis 12 forward. If we continue reading down to Genesis 22:18, the thought of this respect continues. God says He will bless Abraham's seed because he had obeyed God's voice in the events over Isaac's sacrifice. Again, had not Abraham obeyed the voice of God all along? Did he not leave Ur and come to Canaan? Did he not worship God in Canaan and wait for Isaac and on and on? After all of that God does not say, "I know you fear me" or "I have known that

172

you fear me." He says, "*Now*, I know that you fear." There is something important that is happening in the relationship between God and Abraham in this moment. God is not flippantly asking for Isaac's life. There is no randomness in His command. God wants for Abraham to show something about his relationship with God.

What does the word "now" mean there? Regardless of how you couch that word "now", whether it is the beginning of a new relationship or the remembrance of an old relationship, there is a change in the bond between God and Abraham. The word "now" is significant. Something is different. There is a new level, or a new respect for the connection that God and Abraham sustained at that point. Otherwise, you do not say the word "now."

What was different after the offering of Isaac than before the offering of Isaac? The answer is found in the same verse. God says:

He said, "Do not lay your hand on the boy or do anything to him, for now I know that you fear God, seeing *you have not withheld your son, your only son, from me*." (Genesis 22:12)

There is the language from the beginning of the chapter again. Isaac is not just Abraham's son in this encounter with God. Isaac is his "son, his only son." The offering of Isaac was unique. God knows this request is different. This is not a "shirt off your back" request. Asking for Isaac is a request that only a dear friend can ask.

Can you come along and say to Abraham, "Kill Isaac for me"? My guess is that if you did, being thrown out of his house might be the calmest response that you may receive. God made it clear that He understood how much Abraham loved his son. A father's love is not something thrown away lightly. What God is asking is if there is anything special in Abraham's heart that is reserved only for God. There was only one way to test that question. The test is about whether or not there is any portion of Abraham's heart that was given to and reserved for Issac and not for God. God never asked Abraham to give away Isaac for any other man. The highest privilege God could ask of Abraham, He reserved for Himself.

In Abraham's life up to that point, nearly every command came with a promise: "Come and I will bless." There is no promise here, just "Give me." In that command, we find God's prerequisite for friendship. God wants complete, unconditional openness. He knew what Abraham loved more than anything in the world and said, "Give me that." He did not ask for Isaac or explain the reason He wanted Abraham's son. There is no need for explanation between friends. There is no promise of repayment. Friends do not keep score as they give to each other.

The cost of friendship is high. That midnight call to a friend may be asking for so much more than a borrowed car. If you are someone's friend, you have an obligation of intimacy and unrestrained giving. To do anything other than stand with your friend and share yourself, your possessions, your heart, and your whole life would be rightly considered betrayal of a trust. Friendship is more than support or companionship. True and enduring friendship offers complete communion in all of life's trials. Its depth is why sharing it too broadly makes us vulnerable. The cost of friendship is so very high.

God does not take friendship lightly. Abraham is only called God's friend after Isaac is offered on the altar. Before that point, he cannot claim the fullness of that relationship with God. He must show himself worthy of the name. In the beginning of this book, we made the point that *God is not called the friend of Abraham. Abraham is called the friend of God.* This test, the whole journey with Abraham, is not to show God's ability to be open and faithful to Abraham. His life's tests are to show that Abraham holds those qualities with God. Abraham must show that every portion of his life is open to God but not on the promise of blessing and not on the threat of punishment. Both of those are missing in Genesis 22. He must show it simply on the unqualified need of his Friend.

God said, "I need Isaac."

Abraham said, "He's yours."

There is complete communion. There is friendship. After 120 years or so of life, Abraham has that trust in God. God does not have to explain why He needs Isaac. Abraham knows that God would not ask for his son without reason. His confidence is that God would never hurt him or break His promises. In that place, there was no danger in giving his son back to God. Abraham had no reason to guard his heart or be selfish over the love and joy of his life. Everything that he possessed, God could have from him.

I wonder how many resurrections Abraham had seen. There are none recorded in the Bible before Abraham's time. We believe God can and will raise the dead because of the evidence of Scripture. Why should Abraham have believed that about God? None of the dead had ever been raised. To that point in Scripture, the resurrection had never been promised openly. Yet, such was the trust that Abraham had in God's faithfulness that he was able to look past the fear of losing his son to the God that would not ever break His promise to bring a blessing through Isaac.

> By faith Abraham, when he was tested, offered up Isaac, and he who had received the promises was in the act of offering up his only son, of whom it was said, "Through Isaac shall your offspring be named." *He considered that God was able even to raise him from the dead*, from which, figuratively speaking, he did receive him back. (Hebrews 11:17-19)

He considered that God was able to raise Isaac back to life after having been, not just slain, but burnt by fire on the altar. Even imagining the aftermath of the sacrifice is grotesque. But Abraham so trusted his Friend that he moved to light the fire of his sacrifice anyway. He moved without hesitation. Trust in His Friend moved Abraham to go through to the point of completion. He did so simply out of the love and respect he had in his dearest Friend. The cost of friendship is so very high.

Apart from the pureness of trust beating in the heart of a relationship, the ability to believe freely in another has no hope of living. I know, as much as I can know anything on this earth, that my wife would never intentionally hurt me. I know that about Eric and my mother and father and family. I know that about the best of Christians in my life. So long as I do, there is always the hope of friendship and intimacy with all of them. But if that bedrock is ever chipped or broken, the relationships will fail. They may fail fast or slow, but they will fail.

Have you noticed that we are still talking about Abraham's trust in God? Abraham is acting because he trusts in God. All that establishes is what we have known all along: God is worthy of friendship. Abraham can open himself to God because God is worthy of being trusted. That is not and has never been the point that we are trying to understand. We know that God is our friend. Abraham's life and his example are not critical to understanding that. Hundreds of Bible stories from each section of Scripture testify to that.

What Abraham teaches us in a way that is not mentioned about any other single man or woman in the Bible is that he was God's friend. This means that *it is safe for God to give* his all to Abraham. Because Abraham has grown to live and love and think like God, God's gifts will not spoil Abraham. A father cannot give an immature son his inheritance. He would, like the Prodigal, waste it without thought. Only after the son is grown and matured and begins to see the world like the father can the gifts be brought out of the father's trust and given to the heir. He then will take them and use them and grow them and honor the name of the father.

Showing that trustworthiness of character in Abraham is the test of Genesis 22. Is Abraham one with whom God can be open? Is the faith that was born in Genesis 15 finally fulfilled in him? His faith was ready. And because it was, what a blessing God had in store for Abraham and his heirs.

Jesus: The Cost of Friendship

Abraham understood God more than he could have ever known. He knew that God is the "El-Shaddai." What he could not have imagined was the infinite quality of God's power and how that power was going to be demonstrated through his own life. Paul is clear that the plan of redemption in Jesus' coming to the earth and offering salvation to all of man never entered even one man's heart until Jesus fulfilled it.

> But we impart a secret and hidden wisdom of God, which God decreed before the ages for our glory. None of the rulers of this age understood this, for if they had, they would not have crucified the Lord of glory. But, as it is written, "What no eye has seen, nor ear heard, nor the heart of man imagined, what God has prepared for those who love him" – these things God has revealed to us through the Spirit. For the Spirit searches everything, even the depths of God. (1 Corinthians 2:7-10)

How much more prescient does that lack of revelation make Abraham's answer to Isaac's question?

176

> And Isaac said to his father Abraham, "My father!" And he said, "Here am I, my son." He said, "Behold, the fire and the wood, but where is the lamb for a burnt offering?" Abraham said, "*God will provide for himself the lamb* for a burnt offering, my son." So they went both of them together. (Genesis 22:7-8)

Abraham knew nothing of Jesus. He knew nothing of the Passover or the Jewish Day of Atonement. He knew none of the imagery of God's Sacrificial Lamb that would come. All he knew was God. God would supply the offering. God would provide a solution to the apparent lack in man's abilities and preparation. Abraham was right on the day of Isaac's offering.

> He said, "Do not lay your hand on the boy or do anything to him, for now I know that you fear God, seeing you have not withheld your son, your only son, from me." And Abraham lifted up his eyes and looked, and behold, behind him was a ram, caught in a thicket by his horns. And Abraham went and took the ram and offered it up as a burnt offering instead of his son. (Genesis 22:12-13)

More than he intended, his words reached down through time and foreshadowed what God would one day do: "So Abraham called the name of that place, 'The LORD will provide'; as it is said to this day, 'On the mount of the LORD it shall be provided'" (Genesis 22:14).

What I find interesting is that Abraham makes those statements without the text giving any indication that Abraham says them by inspiration. Special revelation was not needed for Abraham to trust in God's providence. He knew his Friend.

Some 1,500 years later, God did provide for himself a Lamb. He offered that Lamb as a sacrifice very nearly on the same spot on which Abraham stood. He opened up Heaven itself. He removed its greatest treasure, its most loved possession. He gave His Son, His only Son, whom He loved, for man.

Paul tells us that He did it for us in a way that no man would have ever done.

> For while we were still weak, at the right time Christ died for the ungodly. For one will scarcely die for a righteous person--

though perhaps for a good person one would dare even to die--
but God shows his love for us in that while we were still
sinners, Christ died for us. (Romans 5:6-8)

He did more than He asked of Abraham. A righteous God asked a man
for his only son. That same God gave His only Son for sinful men.
Why? Did God give to man without the hope of something in return?

I believe Abraham is the key to understanding a portion of that
answer. His life does not direct us to consider man's ability to perform.
His example does not focus us on an answer about his strength or
ability or any of those measurable qualities. We have nothing in those
areas that God wants. We can never hope to please Him in those ways.
Our inevitable struggles with sin makes those terms an untenable basis
for His blessings.

Abraham teaches us another lesson. His life teaches us about the
power of fulfilled faith. The Bible connects Abraham and faith, always.

For if Abraham was justified by works, he has something to
boast about, but not before God. For what does the Scripture
say? "Abraham believed God, and it was counted to him as
righteousness." Now to the one who works, his wages are not
counted as a gift but as his due. And to the one who does not
work but believes in him who justifies the ungodly, his faith is
counted as righteousness, just as David also speaks of the
blessing of the one to whom God counts righteousness apart
from works: "Blessed are those whose lawless deeds are
forgiven, and whose sins are covered; blessed is the man against
whom the Lord will not count his sin." (Romans 4:2-8)

Abraham is the father of all who believe. He is the prototype of our
faith. He shows us what the power of faith can be in our lives.
However, there is something more important. Abraham lived before
God and demonstrated the power of a man's faith. He showed God
that a man's faith is something that can be trusted and that will not be
spoiled if God draws near to bless it.

What did God do for man? He gave His Son. God gave His Son
without question, without qualification, and without any justification.
Man simply needed the best of what God had, and so He gave it to us.

Yet, God's gift was not given without precedent. In the person of Abraham, man had already stood before God and given. Without question, without qualification, and without justification, man gave to God. Man gave his son, his only son, whom he loved to the God that he loved more. In that act, Abraham, our father, showed, not through his perfect works but through his perfect faith, that man can trust God with a whole-hearted perfection. Man can then be trusted in the intimacy of friendship with God. In faith, Abraham showed that a man could love God more than all the world or anyone in it. He showed that a man could love God just as God loves all men.

God's gift of Jesus is more than charity, although it is that. His death for us is more than grace and pity, although it is that. Jesus' death is a testimony of trust from God. It is a gift from one friend to another, between two peers in faithfulness and loyalty. God answered our late-night phone call in distress. In the gift of His Son, God pronounced that He believes in man's heart's potential to come to Him without reservation – just like Abraham has done. Jesus is His testimony that He believes in the heart of the seed of Abraham – you. Your God believes that He can give to you with unrestrained intimacy without your becoming spoiled on His love. He sees in your faith one worthy of being called His friend.

Your Heart: The Cost of Friendship

I admit it. I fail God all the time. I talk too little and too late. I talk too much and too soon. I choose the easy and the wrong far too often. God is not the sole recipient of my shortcomings. I do those things all the time to Julie and to Eric and to my children and my parents and everyone I know. In spite of all those missteps, I still know this: Those people love me. I wrong Julie more than anyone in the world. Her ledger could be full of marks against me. I had a teacher in school who would hug my wife and say, "I'm so sorry," whenever he saw her. He still does it, and it has been two decades since I was there. I think he might be serious. She does not listen to his jokes. There are no marks against me in her book.

Through it all, I have no doubt that she loves me. At the core of her openness to me is that about which we talked earlier. Julie does not trust me for my abilities. Her love is not based in my amazing judgment

179

to pick the right path without fail. What I know she trusts is my heart. My wife knows I would never seek to harm her. In that state, my weak actions can be overlooked.

My guess is that you know exactly those same things about your friends. You do not sit back and keep track of how they have wronged you or injured you. There is no ledger of what they have done wrong to you. You love them because you trust the common values you share in your hearts. As long as that is true, the actions do not matter. Friendship is not based on actions. It is based on trust. There is no need to count who owes whom. Money and deeds have no impact on your balance sheet. I love the Contemporary English Version's translation of 1 Corinthians 13:4-5, "Love is kind and patient, never jealous, boastful, proud, or rude. Love isn't selfish or quick tempered. *It doesn't keep a record of wrongs that others do.*"

"It doesn't keep a record of wrongs that others do." Many might think of the King James' rendering of that phrase, "thinketh no evil." That is the kind of love that is at the heart of friendship. Love does not sit back and record every wrong doing. There is no need. Love trusts that the heart of the other person is not holding anything back. God saw that exact quality in Abraham. Nothing was held back. His actions were not always right, we have seen many wrong steps in his life. But his heart was pure and open.

I have often wondered why we as Christians struggle to allow God to do something that we do with each other so freely. Where do we think that we got the ability to love and trust another? We can have a trust that shares even the most cherished secrets of our hearts, in spite of our misdeeds and wrong actions with each other. Do we think that came from Satan? Or is it more likely that it comes to us because we are made in the image of God? We can fail our friends and spouses and loved ones – repeatedly – and still believe they love us. Because of the power of friendship, we can suffer harm and even betrayal at the hand of a friend and still long for reconciliation. Our longing to be connected with others can overcome the weakness we discover in each other. Again, where did we learn that ability? Is it from God or from Satan?

Who commanded us to love with a love that "doesn't keep a record of wrongs that others do?" The God who is love did. If He commanded it, why do we think that He does not practice it? Yes, a just God practices a love that does not keep a record when His friends do wrong. How is that possible?

The answer is in Abraham. The power of Abraham's faith is that it shows a man is counted as righteous apart from his works (Romans 4:6). What kind of man is that? He is a man like Abraham. He is the man of whom Paul says David was speaking in Psalm 32: "Blessed is the man against whom the LORD counts no iniquity, and *in whose spirit there is no deceit*" (Psalm 32:2).

The man protected from his own sins is the pure hearted man. He is a man who like Abraham holds no part of his heart back from God. This man's heart, his faith, is worthy of being trusted. His actions may fall short. But like a dear friend, God is not counting that man's actions. He is counting the intimacy of his faith.

Still not convinced? Read again Romans 4:8 in its quotation of Psalm 32: "Blessed is the man against whom the Lord *will not count his sin.*"

Would you like to guess the original word that is translated "will not count" in the verse above? Would it surprise you to know that it is the same word found in 1 Corinthians 13:5? The "will not" in Romans 4:8 is the same Greek word that is translated, "doesn't keep a record of" in 1 Corinthians. The same love He commands of us and that we use in exhortation at nearly every wedding to describe the trust and intimacy which the closest friendship of marriage demands, is the same love that God has toward the man in whose "spirit there is no deceit." It is the love expressed to and understood by those who are His friends.

Do you believe that a husband and wife can live without keeping a running tally of every time they have wronged each other? I do. Growing up, I saw it in the life of my mother and father. I see that ability in my wife now. I do not need to beg her to take me back when I fail, nor does she. I have known countless couples that have been married for half a century or more and not a one of them failed in this regard. You find a couple with even a mental ledger of transgressions, and you are looking at a couple doomed to failure.

This love comes from God. God commanded it. However, in practice, we seem to believe that we are better at it than God. We confuse God's holiness with intolerance. He is holy and calls us to holiness (1 Peter 1:15-16). In our minds we connect holiness to maintaining perfect actions in our lives. Yet, our holiness is not founded on perfect action, but on a pureness of heart. Which comes first in the Beatitudes, a "pure heart" or "perfect action?" Strangely, "perfect action" is nowhere to be found in the "Sermon on the Mount." Yes, that perfect heart leads to a perfecting of action, just as a good husband learns over time to treat his wife in a more nearly perfect manner. But that heart and those actions are not the same thing.

Abraham's example is not one that ignores the works that flow from a pure heart. In fact, the passage we have used in this chapter from the book of James speaks of the essential quality of Abraham's works. We are not trying to speak of or justify some kind of excused rebellion. That kind of spirit has deceit in it. God always judges that.

My guess is that a reader of this book is not a rebel against God; he is a maturing or struggling saint. Someone, like you, who is trying to find peace and strength within a committed relationship with God engages in the effort to read something like this. My guess is that you find it hard, at times, to walk with God and accept His love. My last guess is that difficulty is in your life because you are focused on your failures and your actions.

Abraham is speaking to you now. His life is telling you that God trusts your effort and the purity and the integrity of your faith. God is not in Heaven maintaining a ledger of your wrongs. You are the only one doing that. God is your Friend. Will you believe that God wants to be yours? He is ready to welcome you into that most intimate of relationships. All He is asking for is your heart – all of it.

The only question is "Are you holding anything back?" God wants to know, "Is there any portion of your heart; is there any portion of your life that you're holding back from me?" There was a gift that Abraham had reserved that only God could touch. The call of friendship said to Abraham, "If you want to be my friend, you must give that special gift."

What is your gift, buried in the depths of your soul, that you may have never expressed to anyone? There is something about your person, your identity, your personality, your possessions, and your desires; there is something buried within you that maybe your own spouse does not know that you're holding back.

What is it? You cannot be the friend of God until you give it. True friendship means that when you sit down to dinner you don't count the money in each other's wallets. You put all of your treasures and dreams together and say, "These belong to us, together."

The cost to do that is high. It is dangerous, but every friend that you have in your life is your testimony that the cost is worth it. God has given His testimony of what He is willing to share with you to be your Friend. Why not trust Him to love your heart as much as you trust the friends you have in this life? He is more trustworthy than they are. He has already given more than they will ever give to you. All He is asking is for you to open your life to Him in the same way. You can do that with God. You can learn to trust that He loves His friend, in spite of all of your shortcomings. You can be His friend.

11

AM I GOD'S FRIEND?

Fulfill the promise of your faith and you will be God's friend.

Am I God's friend? Even after all that has been written and all the time invested in looking at such an amazing man in Abraham, I have to admit that is a hard question to answer. I know that He is my Friend. But I have known that since page 1. He is the perfect Friend. There is no imperfection in Him in any way that limits His ability to be open to me. The other half of the equation concerning my ability to draw close to Him is always a challenge to understand. The moment I begin to think the answer to that question is "yes," it feels as if the seeds of self-deception have been planted. There is just something unsettling with claiming such an intimate connection with an almighty God.

Before we draw this book to a close, I felt it would be helpful to sharpen the point of the lessons we have drawn from Abraham. When I read a book, I want it to give me something clear and concise to take away from it. For a thought to be powerful, it must be practical. What is the practical point that comes from talking about a "fulfilled faith?" I want to give you five tests you can take from Abraham against which you can examine your faith to tell where you are on the path to friendship.

But first . . .

Perception, not Reality

I want to leave another reminder about the exhortation we are making. The construct that we have used to understand our position before God – that of *servant, steward, son, and friend* – is not intended as a litmus test or even a definite ladder that one climbs in coming closer to God. In the opening pages we stated this construct is not about reality, it is about perception. If one presses that four-part paradigm too hard and too rigidly, it will not sufficiently describe all of the nuances of faith. It is just a tool.

We need to hear again that there is never a time when any one stage mutually excludes another. We are always servants, stewards, sons, and friends. Each of us has areas of strength and weakness. In some ways and on some days, we need God as our Master or Father or Friend. "Friend" Christians are not superior to "Servant" Christians in any real way in relation to their salvation. Coming away from this book with the thought that some are "more saved" than others would be exactly the opposite lesson than it is trying to teach. The lesson is one of intimacy and acceptance that God offers to His people. Our acceptance as His saints is full and complete from day one. The offering of Jesus sealed God's love for us before we ever responded to the gospel.

One of my favorite verses in the Bible is Hebrews 10:14: "For by a single offering he has perfected for all time those who are being sanctified." The thought is wonderful. By His offering, we are perfected forever. Once covered by His blood, since God does not keep a ledger of our wrong in that condition, there is never a moment in time when He sees us as less than perfect. Even while the process of our spiritual growth lingers, we are perfect forever. I believe the power of that offering was effectual even for Abraham. He was counted as righteous in Genesis 15 and remained so through Genesis 22 and beyond. Even before he was called a friend, he was held dear and righteous with God.

I pray that you hear that message. This book is not about your perfection before God. That is not a matter of your performance. That is founded on the power of Jesus' offering. Our message has been focused on how you understand the basis of your perfection while you are growing in your sanctification. I can think of no greater lesson for the saint to learn. If you need to see God as your Master in order to remain faithful, if a close appreciation of His ability to judge is the best motivation you can find to honor Him, there is absolutely nothing wrong with that. You do not need to be fixed. You are not broken. You, living as His humble servant, are perfect in His sight.

This book is not about your salvation. It is about your perception of that salvation.

See God Clearly

My only plea to His servants would be that I pray that you do not continue to live as servants because all you can see is God as a Master. If your faith needs God as a Ruler, then that is wonderful. God will be that for you and love you the whole time. But if you fear Him like the one talent man in that great parable who said of God:

> He also who had received the one talent came forward, saying, "Master, *I knew you to be a hard man*, reaping where you did not sow, and gathering where you scattered no seed, *so I was afraid*, and I went and hid your talent in the ground. Here you have what is yours." (Matthew 25:24-25)

Then I am pleading with you to go back and read Abraham's life and review the material of this book over and again until you can see God as more. Such a harsh and limited view of God cost the one-talent man his life. Such a limited understanding of your God will quite possibly cost you your soul. His holiness is not meanness. He is not a "hard" God – not toward His people.

Abraham's legacy is one of faith that leads to an appreciation of the tender intimacies we can have with God. The "abundant life" promised by Jesus is not one of slavery under the hand of a "hard" God. Jesus' promise is liberty to explore all of the spiritual wonders of this life. There is so much more that God has given to us than we can ever imagine. He is not the limit of our growth. His blessings and love are new every morning. We are the limit of our spiritual growth. God will never say it is time to stop learning and growing. We are not slaves with a small, menial role in His plan. We are even more than children not privileged to know the will of our Father. We are friends, bearing the burden and sharing in the glory.

Now, to the real question: "How can I know that I am God's friend?" Answering the five questions that follow will help you answer that.

Do I Know His Will For Me?

I am always amazed at how often I hear people ask that question. They seem to ask it about every issue of life that arises. I understand and empathize with the feeling which resides in us that spurs that thought on. Consider a quick illustration before we discuss this more.

There was a time in my family's life when, because of work schedules, my wife and I would always take the kids through the drive-through on Wednesday night before our church's mid-week Bible study. With three of them and a budget to meet, most often they were told to order off of the dollar menu. We would get the value items, one huge soda, and five straws. The whole family was fed for around $10. Dad was happy. Our practice trained the kids. Even though they are full-grown now and the family finances are better, they still go to the value menu unless I tell them otherwise. My point is, they now have more freedom than they realize. Their perception is still that of small children. They are stilling looking for me to direct specifically even though I have no preference. I know they will act responsibly now. They can pick the right foods and will not carelessly let things go to waste. When I take them through a drive-through, I have taken them as far as I am trying to direct them. Kids, I have enough money in my wallet, you get what you want.

I fear we do the same thing with God. The Bible says He has given unto us "all things that pertain to life and godliness." Those things are found in His word. The principles for living life and being godly are in Scripture and that is what He wants out of our lives, "For this is the will of God, your sanctification" (1 Thessalonians 4:3). He has given us all the principles and values He deemed necessary to live godly lives.

Still, we want more. We long for Him to show us what to order off of the menu of His blessings. Our hearts want specifics. We want to know where to live and to work and who to love and so on. People look under every rock for a hint from God. God is standing back saying, "I trust you not to waste this life. Go live it in any godly way you wish. You can order whatever you want."

Occasionally, I receive objections from people when talking on this matter. The most common wording of those objections is, "You're taking God away from me." In this teaching, those hearts are hearing a message that sees a God who does not care about the condition of their daily lives. They would feel as if God does not love them if He is unmoved by the struggles and decisions that face them each day.

This message is not about God's love for man. His attitude is not one of apathy. God's attitude toward us is trust. That is exactly the attitude Jesus had with His disciples. Just before His crucifixion, He assured them of His trust in their faith with these words:

> No longer do I call you servants, for the servant does not know what his master is doing; but I have called you friends, for all that I have heard from my Father I have made known to you. (John 15:15)

He said, "I have told you everything there is to know. I have held nothing back. Why? Because you are my friends." From that, He wanted them to understand how to remain faithful.

When God gave us all things that pertain to life and godliness, He told us the same thing. We are no longer servants, who need to be told what to do each day. We are friends, adults in faith, trusted with the principles needed to live as God would live in this world.

The simple reason God does not speak directly from Heaven to you is you do not need it. You should feel empowered from His word to handle the crises of life. A slave needs to be overseen so as not to be lazy. A child needs constant supervision. A friend is a spiritual adult, able to use the truths He has been taught just the way God intended.

What is your attitude toward God's will for you? Can you take God's word and make right choices from the lessons taught in it? Have you conditioned your conscience through the study of His word to respond to challenges with an instinctive godliness?

- **Servants need direction.**
- **Children need experience.**
- **Friends take responsibility.**

Where do you stand?

Do I Obey His Will?

In this last chapter, we talked at length about the amazing power of faith. We discussed the trust that develops in healthy relationships. That trust is needed in each other's hearts to allow true intimacy. We made the point that in those kind of relationships, the individual acts of weakness do not destroy the relationship. True friendship is founded, not on action, but on pureness of heart.

However, action is not unimportant. Action follows heart. A good tree gives good fruit. A bad tree gives bad fruit. Persistent wrong action is not a sign of weakness. When a heart does not move to correct itself, it is a sign of rebellion, callousness, hypocrisy or just apathy. After all, "faith without works is dead." That will always be true.

Here the "once-saved-always-saved" proponents run afoul of scripture. Purity of faith expressed from a spirit in which is "no deceit" (Psalm 32:2) can maintain a relationship with God. Yet, once that spirit is tainted with the stain of "deceit," no longer will it be true that God "will not" count his evil deeds. If there is a man to "whom the Lord will not impute sin," then there is another man to whom He will.

Jesus tied this concept clearly to friendship with these words to His disciples: "You are my friends if you do what I command you" (John 15:14). How much more simply could Jesus have expressed the essential nature of obedience?

I have read long volumes discussing how grace and faith and works and law all come together in God's plan. I do not have all the answers. Men much more learned than I am have struggled with the harmony of those concepts. However, I do know one thing at least. If I have a part of my life that I will not bring in submission to Jesus, if I will not obey Him in every way, I am not His friend.

Part of what we saw in Abraham's life was a man that began to make choices like God. He began to defend righteousness and justice like God would. He did it instinctively and passionately. Having those shared values was part of His growth toward friendship. Is that you? More importantly, do you agree instinctively with what He has commanded? If you are always arguing with Him about the legitimacy of truth, it will be hard to be His friend. Friends live with shared values. Is that true of you and God?

Here is a practical test of friendship:

- **Servants rebel and seek to escape when they can.**
- **Sons need correction and to have each choice explained.**
- **Friends walk with each other because they are united in judgment.**

Where are you?

Why Do I Obey Him?

As important as it is to obey, I think this question might get us closer to the point more quickly. Why you choose to follow God says as much about your perception of Him as anything I know. Read the heading again and answer it with the first thought that comes to mind. Write that thought down. Go back and read Part 1 of this book again. Read the Scriptures which talk of servants, stewards, sons, and friends. Your response is in there somewhere.

- The servant fears punishment – "I don't want to go to hell."
- The steward longs for reward –" I can't wait to go to Heaven."
- The son longs to honor the father – "I want to give glory to God."
- The friend has been transformed to like Him – "It is just who I am."

I love Genesis 18 in this study because it shows that transformation in Abraham. He chides God for indicating that the righteous would be swept away with the innocent. A servant would have never dared to speak for fear of being punished. As Abraham had never been given charge over Sodom, he, as a steward had no reason to voice an opinion. The son might ask why or simply acquiesce to the decree of the father, thinking there was a lesson being taught. But a friend would do what Abraham did. He knew truth. He understood right from wrong on his own. Righteousness was his principle as much as God's. When it was in danger of being broken, Abraham had no choice but to speak even if that meant confronting God. In spite of the specter of punishment, Abraham so valued righteousness, he had to speak.

Why do you obey God? God's work in your life is to transform you just as He did Abraham. He wants you to value for yourself the same things that He values. God wants your thoughts to be like His. Would you, like Abraham, stand up in the defense of the principles of your life even if it were God you believed was going to violate the truths you hold dear?

- **Servants and stewards think of obedience's impact on themselves.**
- **Sons think of obedience's impact on God.**
- **Friends see the worth of obedience in its power to proclaim truth.**

What was your answer?

Do I Feel Unworthy?

"I just hope I can be a janitor in Heaven." I hate that plea. First, it is fairly demeaning of janitors. Secondly, it sounds like humility, but I cannot help but think it is doubt. The statement is dressed-up servanthood. I could add pages and pages to the end of this book listing verses that speak of the crowning of God's saints, of our royal and noble birth, of the grandeur of our inheritance and all of the blessings God has showered down upon His people. I cannot add one letter to this book containing the verses which speak of janitors or street-sweepers or plumbers or any other perceived menial tasks that will be given to us in Heaven. Not only are phrases like that not true humility, but they are also not biblical. The Prodigal came back as a son with a feast and a robe and a ring. God does not need or want you to pick up His garbage.

Why is it that we can come to a verse like Luke 17:10, "So you also, when you have done all that you were commanded, say, 'We are unworthy servants; we have only done what was our duty,'" read one phrase, "unworthy servants," and use that to describe our standing before God, while, at the same time, we ignore verse after verse which speak of us as priests and kings?

My guess is we feel more comfortable as unprofitable servants, more because of our view of God and less because of our view of ourselves. We agree, quietly, with the one-talent man that God is a "hard God." Life hits us hard, and we lose faith. Our children wander from the faith, and we blame ourselves and feel that we have let God down. Our churches whither as they slowly die, and we cannot stop it from happening; so, we wrap ourselves in the same cloak of blame. Life just goes on and on, and we feel powerless to stop it. We feel the burden of lifting God up and cannot see it happening in our lives. Our own insecurities cloud God's face from us so that we cannot see how He could possibly love us.

Do you know whom I seek out when I feel small and weak against the troubles of my life? I go to Julie. It never enters my mind that she will not love me for simply being human. That she will be a shelter for me – without question or reservation – is always my trust. I know that about her because I know her. Julie is good, compassionate, and tender toward me – always. There is no reason to fear her rejection.

Why do I not know that about God? I call Him "my Shepherd," and then doubt it when I fail. Do I really know Him? Do I really trust His love? Do I really believe in the goodness of His nature? Do you?

This is the biggest lesson I want readers to take from Abraham's life. God took a man out of the home of an idolater and walked by his side for a lifetime with one goal for that man's life – to make him His friend. Your start was not too low for His love. The progress of your faith is not too slow for Him to keep walking at your side. You are not unworthy of God.

"The slave does not remain in the house forever; the son remains forever. So if the Son sets you free, you will be free indeed."
(John 8:35-36)

- **Servants fear rejection.**
- **Sons fear disappointing the father.**
- **Friends trust for help in times of trouble.**

Which are you?

Am I Afraid to Dream?

I love this question. Dreams are scary. Solomon felt the fear of an unrewarded dream in his doomed earthly quest for meaning. In that setting, even dreams of godly service were dangerous.

> Be not rash with your mouth, nor let your heart be hasty to utter a word before God, for God is in Heaven and you are on earth. *Therefore let your words be few. For a dream comes with much business*, and a fool's voice with many words. When you vow a vow to God, do not delay paying it, for he has no pleasure in fools. Pay what you vow. It is better that you should not vow than that you should vow and not pay. (Ecclesiastes 5:2-5)

His advice is not to make any vows to God. A dream can only be accomplished if you work hard. If you fail, God will punish you. So it is better not to vow than to vow and fail. Please understand the context of that passage before applying it to you. Solomon is speaking from a very limited perspective. His words are wholly earthly. They should not be yours. Solomon's words are the words of a servant. His thoughts express the fears of our one-talent friend in Matthew 25. His worries should not be yours. You can do better.

To a lesser degree, I believe I have seen Christians with that mentality. They see a place of new challenge or service in their lives and are far too paralyzed by doubt and fear to move. We talked at length about the concept of trading the good for the better and best. We have come back to it again.

Solomon would not advise you to promise God that you will serve Him more because you might fail and God "has no pleasure in fools." That fearful thinking will keep you in a place of comfortable service all your life, but it will let spiritual greatness slip away from you. "Better safe than sorry" is not an acceptable adage for people of faith. Jesus came to free us from that. He brought an abundant life (John 10:10). His work brought the power of life to light in our lives (2 Timothy 1:10).

You should never be afraid to fail while trying to live for God.

The mind of a:

- **Servant says, "If I fail, I will be punished."**
- **Son says, "If I fail, seeing my Father disappointed would hurt too much."**
- **Friend says, "If I fail, I will learn my lesson and try again."**

The servant values his performance. The son values the father's approval. The friend values the loyalty of his fellow-laborer: "For we are fellow-workers with God."

What is holding you back from trying to seize the dream of your heart? Doubt and fear is the diet of the servant's dream. Hope and boldness feed the friend's dream. How hungry is your dream?

You are God's Friend

I wonder, after the events on Mt. Moriah with Isaac, how many more days did Abraham live in which he asked, "Does God love me? Is God pleased with my life?" My guess is zero. The work of his lifetime had completed his faith. He was God's beloved companion into eternity. Abraham was God's friend. Friend means "beloved." God loved Abraham. You are free to be God's friend because God loves and trusts you with that same love.

I want to leave you with this thought at the last. This is not a book about God being your Friend. You need to believe that you are God's friend. I know you value your time of communion with God. You treasure hearing His word and spending time in His presence. There was no need to write the book entitled, "Having God as Your Friend." You already knew that.

You are God's friend and that makes all the difference. God loves you – always. God values His communion with you. He treasures hearing your words and sharing in your life. He rejoices in seeing your dreams being realized. Your Friend welcomes the opportunity to encourage and lift you up when you fail. God longs to spend time in the presence of His friend: you.

Accept that thought, and it can change your life. You can live a life without fear and doubt. The comfort of friendship with God will not remove pain or trouble, but it will forever eliminate your need to wonder what you have done to anger God when those things come. Friends do not treat each other like that.

How many more days will you live asking those same questions of doubt: "Does God love me? Is he pleased with my life?" God loves you as much as He loved Abraham. He is working in your life to complete your faith. It is time to walk with Him from Ur to Moriah. It is time to give up the "good" for the "best." It is time for your faith to be completed. The time to become God's friend is now. Your faith fulfilled makes you God's friend.

WORKS CITED

Bauer, Walter, William F. Arndt, and F. Wilbur Gingrich. *A Greek-English Lexicon of the New Testament and Other Early Christian Literature.* 4th rev. and augm. ed. Chicago: University of Chicago Press, 1957. Print.

Earle, Ralph. *Word Meanings in the New Testament.* Peabody, Mass.: Hendrickson, 1997. Print.

Free, Joseph P. *Archaeology and Bible History.* Ed. Howard F. Vos. Grand Rapids, Mich.: Zondervan, 1992. Print.

Keil, Carl Fredrich, and Franz Delitzsch. *Commentary on the Old Testament in ten volumes.* Grand Rapids, MI: Eerdmans, 1986. Print.

Pfeiffer, Charles F. *Baker's Bible Atlas.* Grand Rapids, Mich., Baker, 1979. Print.

Pfeiffer, Charles F., Howard F. Vos, and John Rea. *Wycliffe Bible Dictionary.* Peabody, Mass.: Hendrickson, 1998. Print.

Scofield, C. I. The Scofield Reference Bible. New York. Oxford University Press American Branch, 1909. Print.

Trench, R. C. *Synonyms of the New Testament.* Peabody, Mass.: Hendrickson , 2000. Print.

ABOUT THE AUTHOR

Jonathan Jenkins is the pulpit minister for the Katy church of Church in Katy, Texas. He has been in the ministry for twenty years and has served churches in Georgia, Mississippi, and Texas. He is a graduate of Freed-Hardeman University and of the Memphis School of Preaching. He and his wife Julie have three children: Austin, Amanda, and Andrew.

Made in the USA
Middletown, DE
17 April 2017